"Irene Yuan Sun provides a memorable and challenging narrative of the industrialization of Africa and the China-Africa relationship, two of the most important trends in development today. Combining first-person research, a deep understanding of development theory, and an encyclopedic grasp of the African landscape, this is the one book to read if you want to understand both the opportunities and the hard choices Africa faces."

—**JONATHAN WOETZEL**, Senior Partner, McKinsey & Company

"Irene Yuan Sun uses vivid stories of private Chinese entrepreneurs in Africa to make complex topics of development, investment, governance, and public health accessible and compelling to the reader. This is a refreshing and beautifully written book."

—**WILLIAM C. KIRBY**, T. M. Chang Professor of China Studies, Harvard University

"By shifting the focus from Chinese trade to productive investment in Africa, Irene Yuan Sun opens a critical frontier with potentially profound impact. This is a pathfinding book that should inspire more work."

—**MUKHISA KITUYI**, Secretary-General, United Nations Conference on Trade and Development

"Irene Yuan Sun is a remarkable and astute observer, and her refreshing and exciting perspective on the new Africa is well worth reading—and remembering."

—**RICHARD LEAKEY**, world-renowned paleoanthropologist and conservationist

"There are very few scholars who understand the nuances of Africa's complicated relationship with China as Irene Yuan Sun does. In a writing style full of flair and dynamism, she provides thorough analysis and relevant insights to help readers understand Africa's industrialization journey and the role China plays in it."

—**ISAAC K. FOKUO JR.**, cofounder, Sino Africa Center of Excellence Foundation; founder and principal, Botho Limited; and former CEO, African Leadership Network

THE
NEXT FACTORY
OF THE WORLD

THE
NEXT FACTORY
OF THE WORLD

HOW CHINESE INVESTMENT
IS RESHAPING AFRICA

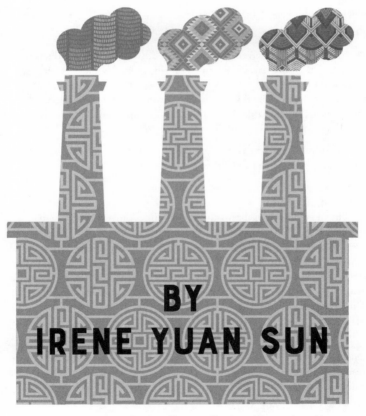

BY
IRENE YUAN SUN

Harvard Business Review Press • Boston, Massachusetts

The web addresses referenced in this book were live and correct at the time of the book's publication but may be subject to change.

Library of Congress Cataloging-in-Publication Data
Names: Sun, Irene Yuan, author.
Title: The next factory of the world : how Chinese investment is reshaping Africa / by Irene Yuan Sun.
Description: Boston, Massachusetts : Harvard Business Review Press, [2017]
Identifiers: LCCN 2017016533 | ISBN 9781633692817 (hardcover : alk. paper)
Subjects: LCSH: Investments, Chinese—Africa. | Manufacturing industries—Africa. | Factories—Africa. | Africa—Economic conditions—1960- | China—Foreign relations—Africa.
Classification: LCC HD9737.A352 S86 2017 | DDC 338.4096—dc23 LC record available at https://lccn.loc.gov/2017016533

ISBN: 978-1-63369-281-7
eISBN: 978-1-63369-282-4

For Merry, who believed as if it were obvious

CONTENTS

A NOTE ON NAMES

Names in this book are generally introduced in the full form if known. Thereafter, each person is referred to as I would address him or her in real life. Hence some people are referred to by English first names; others by Mr. or Mrs. followed by the family name; still others by their full names, as is Chinese custom between people of similar ages. I have occasionally changed names or redacted them altogether to protect people's privacy; such cases are noted.

From the Current Factory of the World to the Next Factory of the World

I remember the first time I rode in a car. Not many people in America can say that, cars being as prosaic as they are here. But this was in China, where I was born and where I lived until age six. Up to that moment, my conception of the Chinese word *qiche* consisted entirely of crowded buses onto which I was squeezed by my parents and heavy-duty trucks that children were definitely not allowed in. This car was something very different: there was no one in it I didn't know, and everything was effortlessly clean. The leather of the seats was smooth and cool to the touch and gave off the calming, sterile smell of newness. I was used to having to clutch my parents' hands on standing-room-only buses or to wrap my arms around their midsections as they pedaled a bicycle. None of that was necessary here, so I wasn't quite sure what to do with the unexpected freedom of my limbs. I wanted to rub the dark-tinted windows to see if they would get lighter so that I could look outside. But I had been told it was a special occasion to sit in such a *qiche*, which probably meant I should keep my hands to myself.

Our family did not own the car, of course. It was the early 1990s, and almost no one in China owned a car. We took a spin in it as a treat from a family friend who was a government official. Four linked rings declared the car to be an Audi—one of the few models that existed in China at that time, and for years afterward the only car brand I could name. China had four carmakers in total, all founded in the 1950s in a fit of central-government-directed investment in heavy industry. The Soviet Union had advised that one of the firms be based in my hometown of Changchun because of its proximity to eastern Russia, the theory being that this nascent car plant could learn from its Soviet counterparts. The resulting firm, FAW, mainly made giant industrial trucks, and over the years, its blue and white logo became ubiquitous around town. But by the time I got to sit in one of its cars, the Chinese government had long ago severed any cooperation, in automobiles or otherwise, with the Soviet Union. In 1990, FAW turned instead to Volkswagen for investment and technical help in a joint venture agreement. FAW continued to make industrial trucks, but it also started making sedans under Volkswagen's Audi brand. That's how it came to be that a year or so later, my family—father, mother, daughter—was sitting together in a car for the first time.

It bears repeating that this happened just twenty-five years ago. I'm only thirty, but I personally witnessed a time when China's now car-clogged streets were full of bicycles instead. Such has been the rapidity of China's transformation, sparked by the rise of Factory China. In the quarter century since I first sat in that car, China has gone from producing 2 percent of global manufacturing output to 25 percent.[1] Over that time China's GDP grew thirtyfold, and 750 million people were lifted out of poverty—the most ever achieved in a single period in the history of the world. China went from being poorer than Kenya, Lesotho, and Nigeria to rivaling the United States for the title of largest economy in the world.[2] But as impressive as these statistics are, to me, the real signs of development are all the small, everyday occurrences that can only delight people who have known life without them. My favorites: Sprite is no longer considered a rare treat, just a mundane soft drink. People now stand in lines at the airport instead of jostling one another relentlessly. Stores now provide toilet paper in their bathrooms. And no one thinks it's anything special to ride in a car anymore.

As these changes were unleashed by China becoming the current Factory of the World, I grew up in the United States, and then went to live in another part of the world. After college, I taught eighth- and ninth-graders in a village in Namibia, in southwestern Africa. During a staff meeting, the principal of my school strong-armed me into running the school shop. Having no clue as to what I should be selling there, I asked at the end of one of my classes if any students would like to go with me—in my car—to the wholesaler an hour away to buy things for the shop. A burst of shouts was accompanied by an eruption of arms into the air. Every single kid wanted to go. More than a few trailed me home, begging me to pick them. I thought it was funny—and familiar. I knew this longing to sit in a car, and the novelty of actually doing so. Cars—and Sprite and toilet paper—may sound like very materialistic ways of defining development, but people who have these things tend to forget how much they are markers of modernity to those who don't. Americans and Europeans can be casual about sitting in a car, but to my child self in China, and to my students in Namibia, it was a thrill. The appearance of such material goods in a society heralds the possibility that people can adopt new selves, new ways of being in the world: as consumers and producers in the modern global economy.

As a volunteer teacher, I was responsible for five classes of math and English in a public school in rural Africa. Nothing is less controversial than the inherent goodness of teaching children and the notion that an educated citizenry is essential for a country's development. But several months into my job, when I was brutally honest with myself, I could see no connection between my daily work and the chance that these bigger transformations would occur. Most of my pupils were the children of subsistence farmers, and the vast majority of them would become subsistence farmers themselves. Some days, the absurdity of what I was doing would hit me: I was teaching irregular English verb conjugations to future subsistence farmers living in an arid plain where no one spoke English in everyday life. I spent a year bearing witness to the things that are wrong and unfair in our world today—children dealing with the brunt of HIV/AIDS, environmental degradation, poverty—and I had nothing to offer. The idea that education was the key to my kids' future seemed empty. That felt sacrilegious at the time, but I sensed that my teaching reinforced rather than expanded the ways in which Africa relates to the world. Receiving wisdom from foreigners who supposedly know better: it's an old trope, dating back at least to European colonial ideology in Africa, and it has never worked. What else would it take for African countries to pull off the transformation I had seen China make in my short lifetime?

Strangely, it was on a blind date that I began to encounter a new reality. A Chinese man from whom I regularly bought vegetables insisted that I come over for dinner one weekend to meet his "good friend." I agreed, mostly to stay on good terms with my vegetable dealer. His friend turned out to be a self-made Chinese man who had come to Namibia at age seventeen and founded a string of successful businesses. He was nearing thirty, rich, and wanted to find a wife, yet very few Chinese women would agree to live in Africa. He did his best to impress me with fresh seafood that he'd arranged to be trucked in sixteen hours from the ocean, but it soon became clear that he was illiterate. It didn't help when he and all his friends pulled out their guns at dinner. The conversation—boisterous, over cases of beer—revealed that he was like many other Chinese businessmen in Africa: a pure capitalist, with seemingly little regard for the welfare or rights of locals. And yet I was struck that this man might end up doing more to help the people in my village than my own well-intentioned efforts. I taught children skills that were theoretically useful for a way of life that no one here actually lived. He created real jobs with real paychecks. In so doing, and probably without meaning to, he opened up new ways of relating to the world for thousands of Africans: as workers, as clients, as partners, even as worthy adversaries. Which one of us was making a difference for Africa?

This is not a romance story—I never saw the man again—but that seed of a question stayed with me. It eventually led me to spend years studying Chinese investment in Africa, knocking on countless factory doors, sweet-talking reticent Chinese owners into letting me onto the premises, and cajoling them into trusting me with their stories. I've visited more than fifty Chinese factories in Africa and talked to numerous Chinese businesspeople involved in other African sectors, along with a hundred-odd African workers, entrepreneurs, government officials, journalists, and union organizers who are partnering with and responding to Chinese interest in their countries in a variety of ways.

It was on one of these research trips in eastern Nigeria that I had my *aha!* moment. At the end of a long, hot day of visiting factories, I showed up at the address of my last appointment and found myself in a courtyard ringed by buildings painted blue and white. The blue of the walls matched the blue of the heavy industrial trucks parked in the courtyard, and something about that blue tugged at a half-buried memory. All in a rush, I realized that this blue felt familiar because it wasn't just any blue—it was FAW blue. I was standing in a brand-new FAW truck factory in Africa.

FAW had come a long way since I first sat in one of its cars, twenty-five years earlier. It had sold 18 million cars and counting in seventy countries, and employed 120,000 people in the process.[3] That awkward child of Sino-Soviet planning, saved by German investment, was now all grown up and building factories in Africa.

Chinese factories in Africa: This is the future that will create broad-based prosperity for Africans and usher in the next phase of global growth for a large swath of the Chinese economy. This is what will make Africa rich and achieve a dramatic and lasting change in living standards. To be clear, Africa today is not defined by poverty: it is characterized by promise and optimism, with eight of the ten fastest-growing economies in the world over the next decade projected to be on the continent.[4] But just as it is wrong to cast Africa in the tired stereotype of pitiful, hopeless destitution, it is problematic to ignore the fact that more than half a billion of the poorest people in the world still live in Africa. Over the past half century, Africa has been the premier testing ground for multiple waves of Western ideas about poverty alleviation. To be sure, Western development programs that help with things like educating children are important for other reasons, but they will not create 100 million jobs and lift half a billion people out of poverty. If we are serious about raising living standards across this vast region of the world, it is time to try something new. That something new has already started moving to Africa: factories.

Factories are the bridge that connects China, the current Factory of the World, to Africa, the next Factory of the World. Over the past fifteen years, Chinese factories have been driven out of China by rising costs, and many have landed in Africa. Chinese companies made a mere two investments in Africa in 2000; they now make hundreds each year.[5] I recently co-led a large-scale research project on Chinese investment in Africa at the global management consulting firm McKinsey; our fieldwork in eight African countries uncovered more than fifteen hundred Chinese firms engaged in manufacturing.[6] Some of these companies are attracted by the rapidly growing domestic markets in countries like Nigeria, which will have a population larger than that of the United States by 2050. Carmakers, construction materials producers, and light manufacturers of consumer goods are all entering the market, hoping for their share of the opportunity. Other Chinese firms have a different business model: they take advantage of Africa's comparatively low labor costs to produce goods for export to developed markets. In Lesotho, Chinese garment factories make yoga pants for Kohl's, jeans for Levi's, and athletic wear for Reebok. Almost all of Lesotho's production is trucked out and packed onto container ships bound for American consumers.

This movement of factories matters, because when factories arrive en masse, prosperity soon follows. From Great Britain at the dawn of the Industrial Revolution in the eighteenth century, to America in the nineteenth century, to Japan and other Asian countries in the twentieth, factories have restructured entire economies toward a new, lasting level of wealth. That's because manufacturing, unlike agriculture and services, engages mass labor in highly productive ways to participate in the global economy. It's also because on an individual level, industrialization allows subsistence farmers enmeshed in highly local systems of exchange to transform themselves into consumers and producers in the global economy. Industrialization is how China reshaped itself from a poor, backward country into one of the largest economies in the world in less than three decades. By becoming the next Factory of the World, Africa can do the same.

To be clear, the rise of manufacturing is not an altogether happy story. Up close, it's often ugly. Some of the Chinese factory bosses I've met in Africa are truly unsavory. Many are racist, and many wouldn't hesitate to pay a bribe. More than a few spit in public, drink to excess, and frequent prostitutes. And their actions have consequences: as the stories in this book show, their bribes affect the proper functioning of local governments, their factories' environmental practices affect the quality of Africa's air and water, and their treatment of employees determines not only the wages of workers but in some cases whether they live or die on the job. China itself—with its corruption scandals and thick, smog-ridden air—provides ominous examples of the social and environmental consequences of unbridled economic expansion. Industrialization unleashes powerful new forces for harm as well as for good, and these are already evident in Africa today.

Although industrialization in Africa will certainly have a dark side, another certainty is that the continent will experience industrialization differently than China did. African countries and societies do not resemble China, economically, politically, or socially. Although factories in any new place lead to a set of predictable changes—from rising incomes to labor scandals—the form, sequence, and flavor of these changes vary considerably. In Nigeria, the course of industrialization is shaped by reports from a free press; in Lesotho, by a strong union movement; in Kenya, by tribal and ethnic loyalties—all of which are largely absent in China. Indeed, in the encounter between Chinese investors and a whole host of local African actors—workers, suppliers, distributors, governments, media—new types of organizations, partnerships, and power structures will be invented. Through this process, Africa has the chance not only to repeat the sort of industrialization that has come before, but to improve on it—if this can't obliterate the seemingly unavoidable trade-offs between development and democracy, economic growth and environmental health, then perhaps it can at least make them less stark. The theme may be old, but the story will be new.

This book is about that story, and it is divided into two parts. Part one is about the *realities* of what it looks and feels like to be inside Chinese factories in Africa, and part two is about the *possibilities*—economic, political, and social—that these factories are unleashing. Part one starts with the basics of Chinese manufacturing investment in Africa: what sorts of factories exist, who owns them, what they make, how they came to be there, how they make money. We will meet the Chinese entrepreneurs who run these factories and understand the business models that have allowed them to thrive so far from home. Despite the current hype about the rise of robotics and the possibility of fully automating production, the classic factory model, in which real people make tangible goods, is far from dead. There's still lots of money to be made with this way, and this business logic is what drives Chinese factory owners to Africa. By and large, these manufacturing entrepreneurs have little to do with the massive tranches of Chinese government–led investment and aid in Africa that the Western press often reports on in tones of fear and incredulity.[7] These private investors care little about geopolitics. They are instead driven by the economics of their individual businesses and the momentum of their own remarkable life trajectories. They are the living incarnation of what's known as the flying geese theory, which predicts that industrialization will occur when groups of factories move from one country to another, like geese migrating across long distances. These are daring undertakings in which entrepreneurs risk their life savings—and sometimes their lives—in foreign lands where they barely speak the language or understand the culture. The entrepreneurs I met are tough, gritty, unglamorous people living out adventure stories—a reminder that the boldest forms of entrepreneurship exist far from the air-conditioned offices of Silicon Valley.

Part two explores the *possibilities* that industrialization is bringing to Africa: full employment, a new crop of homegrown factory owners, a more effective set of institutions, a path to prosperity for the marginalized. These are actualities that other regions of the world have achieved through industrialization. For Africa, at this early date, there are no assurances yet, but there are already many beginnings. From these beginnings, we can sense that development is not linear, clean, or predictable. This challenges our notion that development should be planned, coordinated, and monitored by authoritative bodies such as the United Nations or aid organizations or even well-functioning governments. The lives of the Africans we'll meet—from workers doing shifts on the assembly line to high-level government officials crafting national policy—show that industrialization is a process that is experienced, negotiated with, and enacted, all at the same time. These are people whose lives are being circumscribed by new forces even as they are being opened to new possibilities. We'll meet a woman going to work for the first time, an entrepreneur desperately trying to fulfill his first big customer order, a government official trying to serve his fellow citizens in a new way. Each reaches for new possibilities, even as new pressures and new restrictions—an unfair boss, an unreasonable customer, a demanding investor—bear down hard. Some succeed; many fail. Their efforts are by turns courageous and pitiful, charmed and doomed, unbelievable in the best and worst ways. This is what it means to *live* industrialization—a process at once marred by uncertainty but guided by hope.

Within its two-part structure, this book delves into four countries in particular: Nigeria, Lesotho, Kenya, and Ethiopia. I'll bring in continent-wide statistics throughout the book, but it's the stories from these four very different countries that will allow us to understand Africa's vast diversity without losing the specificity of its characters. Nigeria is a behemoth by any standard: it has the largest population and the largest economy on the continent. It is perhaps best described by native son Chinua Achebe: "strongly multiethnic, multilingual, multireligious, somewhat chaotic."[8] Oil dominates Nigeria's economy, but its irrepressible entrepreneurial spirit can be seen everywhere and in everyone, from street vendors who miraculously materialize at every traffic jam to Nigerian-born Aliko Dangote, the richest man in Africa. Responsiveness to consumer needs is the name of the game for Chinese factories in Nigeria, as Chinese entrepreneurs target ever-lower price points to access mass markets.

Some 4,500 miles away, tucked into the highlands of southern Africa, tiny Lesotho is nearly the polar opposite of Nigeria in every way. Landlocked and completely surrounded by its much larger neighbor, South Africa, it has few natural resources and a population of only 2 million. With these scare resources, it has to contend with the third-highest rate of HIV infection in the world.[9] But even here, Chinese factories have found a niche due to Lesotho's favorable position under US trade policy. As a result, Lesotho has become a link in the global supply chain that churns out the yoga pants and T-shirts ubiquitous in the United States.

A world apart from both Nigeria and Lesotho, Kenya is the flagship economy of East Africa, boasting its own brand of entrepreneurship and innovation. Although youth unemployment has been worrisome and security concerns about neighboring Somalia lurk, Kenya's GDP has grown consistently at a robust 5–6 percent a year over the past five years, and its burgeoning tech sector has earned Nairobi the moniker "Silicon Savannah." Here, more than a few Chinese companies are attempting to innovate as well, introducing new technologies to the Kenyan market and experimenting with novel partnerships with the local government.

Finally, to the north of Kenya, in the Horn of Africa, lies proud Ethiopia, the only African country never to have been colonized by a European power. Yet its 100 million people have spent the past twenty-five years rebuilding from a convulsive decade of famines and "Red Terror" inflicted by a brutal Marxist dictatorship in the 1970s. Ethiopia today is transitioning to a market economy in a piecemeal way, with strict capital controls and state monopolies over many industries that call to mind no other country so much as China. It is no wonder that Chinese companies feel at home here, building special economic zones and investing in sectors deemed priorities by the Ethiopian government.

Taken together, these four countries by no means constitute a representative picture of Africa, but they do give a flavor across several important dimensions: big, medium, and small countries; eastern, western, and southern Africa; resource-rich, resource-poor, and somewhere-in-between economies. Despite these different contexts, one thing is common: Chinese factories are taking root. We need to pay attention.

That day, when I stood in the courtyard of the FAW factory, I was humbled. I had dedicated my life to development work—teaching kids, consulting for donors and global aid organizations. Yet ever since that strange dinner in Namibia with the self-made Chinese man, I had been questioning whether these would matter in the grand scheme of things. They were necessary and good and perhaps even noble for a host of reasons, but they will not develop Africa. Standing inside that blue-and-white factory with machines roaring to life, I finally understood that the future of Africa depends on industrialization. This is what will allow Africa to follow in the footsteps of Japan, South Korea, Taiwan, and China: to employ its booming population, to grow world-class firms, to raise living standards across the bulk of its populace. If Africa can lift just half as many people out of extreme poverty as China did in a mere three decades, it would be eliminated from the continent.[10] For nearly 400 million people, this would mean the difference between going hungry and being full, between looking for work and holding down a job, between asking their children to work at menial jobs and sending them to school. This would be a human accomplishment of the highest order.

In this historical moment, in which China has taken the lead on reshaping the global development apparatus by creating $250 billion worth of new development institutions (including, literally, the New Development Bank), it bears remembering that Development with a capital "D" has rarely permeated daily life pervasively enough to warrant being described as development with a lowercase "d." That is to say, if these new institutions are truly to reinvent the way we collectively help poor countries achieve prosperity, they need to rediscover that development is at its heart about industrialization. Development institutions can certainly play an important role in accelerating industrialization in Africa and in easing the transition for many Africans, but they won't be the ones who will do the heavy lifting. Instead, what matters most for Africa's future is the work of people who don't think they are doing development at all: the rough-hewn Chinese boss who came to Africa just to get rich, the scrappy African worker who starts doing odd jobs and rises to manage the whole plant. Their efforts are permanently restructuring African economies for high-productivity manufacturing, which will do for poverty alleviation, education, and health in Africa what a half century of well-intentioned aid efforts have not. These people are sparking an industrial revolution in Africa, one that will allow Africa to take over from China as the Factory of the World. Let's meet some of them.

PART ONE

REALITIES

CHAPTER 1

A Human Chain Reaction

Mr. Sun insisted that we have tea. My fellow researcher and I had already seen his ceramics plant—earlier, the manager had taken us through the factory and explained the workings of the machinery and the logic of the business. But Mr. Sun had just returned to Nigeria from a trip back to China, and he had a batch of top-quality green tea that he wanted to share with his visitors, in an age-old gesture of Chinese hospitality.

He ushered us into his office and motioned us toward a plump sofa. We had had tea the previous morning with another Chinese manufacturer down the road, sitting on low-slung stools in the weedy yard of his factory and drinking lukewarm brownish liquid poured from a cracked teapot. Mr. Sun clearly had something different in mind. He set out a proper Chinese tea-making set, with a polished wooden tray and separate containers for steeping, rinsing, discarding, and enjoying the tea. He chatted away as his hands expertly went through the intricate steps of tea preparation. His words, too, followed a ritual: he was so honored to receive us; he relished having visitors from Tsinghua and Harvard, since he himself was only an elementary school graduate who had started working at age thirteen; he hoped that we would look kindly on his humble factory. Meanwhile, that so-called humble factory hummed along in the building next door, producing 56,000 square meters of ceramic tile—enough to cover ten football fields—a day. Inside the office, Mr. Sun raised the first steep of fine tea to his nose; like a connoisseur enjoying the bouquet of a rare wine, he closed his eyes, inhaled, and then poured the entire contents into the discard drain. Classic Chinese tea etiquette holds that the first pour is too sharp, too dirty, to drink, so the finest teas are drunk only after a second steep. A few moments later, the tea was ready. Mr. Sun poured us each a tiny cup. We smelled the delicate aroma, then sipped carefully.

High-end Chinese teas are meant to be drunk over the course of as many as a dozen pours, with each steep producing a slightly new experience to be savored. It was clear that Mr. Sun intended his tea to be enjoyed thus, so we settled in for what would surely be another hour or two. At the second or third pour, we were still on the ritual niceties—we complimenting Mr. Sun on his factory and his tea; Mr. Sun insisting that he did not deserve such praise. By the fourth or fifth pour, we had run out of small talk, and Mr. Sun became reflective. He started telling us his life story, almost fable-like in its contours: a poor, uneducated Chinese boy works hard, eventually becomes his own boss, and gets rich.

Mr. Sun's story is a rags-to-riches story about an individual's rise, but it's also a story about the industrialization of nations. The shift toward working in factories, running factories, and owning factories is a macroeconomic process that has transformed China over the past generation and is on the cusp of unleashing great changes in Africa as well. As we shall see, Mr. Sun in many ways embodies China's remarkable development path from the 1970s to today—the fastest rise in living standards in recorded human history. That rise was possible precisely because China did not follow the orthodox advice of Western development institutions but instead created the conditions for Mr. Sun and a generation of his counterparts to work in factories and learn to run them. Many did so by working for Taiwanese factory owners, who in turn had learned from Japanese ones. This trajectory suggests that industrial development is not a self-generated phenomenon, but rather a chain reaction ignited from one country to another. And the indispensable vector at the heart of this transformation is nothing so grand as capital or so abstract as technology. It is human beings. The beneficiaries of someone who decided to put a factory in their country, human beings such as Mr. Sun become the living embodiment of accumulated manufacturing know-how. And when they decide where to put their next factory, they are choosing the next link in the chain of manufacturing. A generation ago, they chose China and transformed it in their wake. Today, they are choosing Africa.

Back in his office in Nigeria, at the eighth or ninth pour of his truly excellent tea, Mr. Sun was waxing philosophical: "The train of development—which station first and then which station you need to go through—we Chinese know exactly what the path is. Nigeria needs to learn from China! For Africa, the Western path is unwalkable."

. . .

Mr. Sun can be considered more of an authority than most on how to get rich. He started life poor, barely had an education, but got rich before he got bald. His strategy has been simple: learn how to make things, make them, and sell them. The way he characterizes China's development path is what he himself has done again and again: make money by building factories. To him, it's obvious that Africans should do the same.

This strategy that Mr. Sun laid out—and lived out—is not unique to China. In fact, after Britain became the first country to generate rapid economic growth on the back of what was then the greatest manufacturing sector in the world, most nations that joined its ranks did so by shifting their economic structure toward industry before transitioning to services. The few exceptions are countries like Qatar that have lucked into extraordinary resource wealth, far beyond even the proportions of amply resource-endowed countries such as Russia and Angola. Globally, there is a strong linkage between industrialization and economic growth: a United Nations analysis of 131 developing countries found a strong correlation between economic growth and manufacturing value addition.[1] This correlation is even stronger for sub-Saharan Africa than for the rest of the world. And economists have shown that modern manufacturing is the only sector in which poor countries have consistently managed to catch up to rich ones in productivity. As the Harvard economist Dani Rodrik writes, "This is a rather remarkable result. It says that modern manufacturing industries converge to the global productivity frontier regardless of geographical disadvantages, lousy institutions, or bad policies."[2] Moreover, this convergence happens regardless of time period or region, and studies have found that Africa is no exception.[3] The accumulated history of countries around the world turns out to be exactly what Mr. Sun intuited: if you want to get rich, build yourself a manufacturing industry.

It is worth noting that this advice is very different from what mainstream development institutions have been dispensing to poor countries for the past two generations. In the 1980s and 1990s, expert advice converged around the Washington Consensus. Influenced by the Ronald Reagan–Margaret Thatcher push for bigger roles for markets and smaller roles for government, the Washington Consensus advocated a sharp curb on government spending and involvement in shaping markets. Its pillars included ensuring macroeconomic stability, cutting subsidies, deregulating markets, privatizing national companies, and liberalizing trade—as Rodrik summarizes it: "Stabilize, privatize, and liberalize."[4] International financial institutions such as the International Monetary Fund and the World Bank played a large role in crystallizing this package into mainstream orthodoxy and guaranteeing its implementation, often by making much-needed economic assistance to developing countries conditional on their agreement to these prescriptive reforms. As we will see in the next chapter, Nigeria was among the many countries in Africa that endured the harsh consequences of these structural transformation programs.

Meanwhile, on the other side of the world, after Mao died in 1976, China embarked on a very different development path. Mr. Sun is from Wenzhou, a midsize city in southeastern China. Wenzhou is famous for inventing a lustrous, pale-green glaze called celadon nearly 4,000 years ago—a discovery that spawned dynasties' worth of elegant Chinese ceramics of the sort found in art museums the world over. In the late 1970s, Wenzhou was again first in China: this time, first in the now-communist country to set up private enterprises. In keeping with the times, Mr. Sun dropped out of school at age thirteen and started working in factories. He worked his way up in several leather-processing plants, eventually saving enough to own one. He was among thousands of Chinese who did the same—working long hours, saving scrupulously, and then using that accumulated knowledge and savings to become factory bosses themselves.

On the global level, it was clear by the mid-2000s that the Washington Consensus had failed. Even the coiner of the term admitted in 2002 that "[t]he results have been disappointing, to say the least, particularly in terms of growth, employment, and poverty reduction."[5] To make matters worse, the implementation of Washington Consensus policies contributed to growing inequality within countries and to increasingly frequent financial crises.[6] Rodrik wrote in 2006, "Proponents and critics alike agree that the policies spawned by the Washington Consensus have not produced the desired results. The debate now is not over whether the Washington Consensus is dead or alive, but over what will replace it."[7]

Over the past decade, the monolithic orthodoxy of the Washington Consensus has splintered into several camps that, while not directly contradicting one another, emphasize differing ingredients as being critical to success in development. Some, like Daron Acemoglu, an influential development economist at MIT, emphasize the quality of governance and institutions. Meanwhile, funding and attention among practitioners in the development community has shifted toward service delivery: getting tangible aid to those who need it most. This is exemplified by the eight Millennium Development Goals spearheaded by the United Nations and championed by other global donors that put primary emphasis on measurable outcomes in health and education. And within Africa, there has been considerable buzz about the notion of *leapfrogging*—or as *Forbes* put it, "the promise that Africa, thanks to the rise of new technology and access to telecoms and internet, would rapidly reach a 'tipping point' that would dramatically accelerate development by enabling trade and entrepreneurship amongst its populations."[8] According to this theory, countries can leap from an agriculture-based economy directly to high-value-added services, bypassing the classic manufacturing-intensive stage of development.

Meanwhile, Mr. Sun continued to manufacture leather goods in China, oblivious of and impervious to these debates raging in the rarefied halls of the World Bank in Washington, DC, and the United Nations in Geneva. Eventually, his business went global. In the late 2000s, costs in China were climbing at an alarming pace, and Mr. Sun realized he needed to move his factory abroad. But where? He considered Bangladesh, then Uzbekistan. Then a friend told him about Nigeria.

He went for a five-day visit. "I got off the plane, and immediately all these poor people were asking for money," he recounts. "But then I realized there were a lot of rich people, too, and although it's hard to make it in this market, I realized that it's just as hard for everyone else as it is for me to make a factory here."[9] Back in China, he called a contact at the customs authority and asked him what was the physically heaviest product being shipped in large quantities to Nigeria. The answer? Ceramics.

There is a certain pleasing aptness that a native son of Wenzhou, the birthplace of ceramics, discovered ceramics as his worldly calling. After that single visit to Nigeria, Mr. Sun devoted nearly $40 million to building a ceramic tile factory there. His factory runs 24/7 and employs nearly 1,100 workers, a thousand of whom are locals. Electricity is unreliable and costly, but business is good. Nigeria, with its relative lack of competition and booming demand, allows Mr. Sun to earn a 7 percent profit margin, compared with the 5 percent he earned in China. In the manufacturing business, margins are often razor-thin; a 2 percent bump is substantial. And that is why, in the middle of the Nigerian bush, an uneducated Chinese man could serve us some of the finest tea on earth.

. . .

What makes these entrepreneurs so willing to move to an unfamiliar land with a foreign tongue and an alien culture? One answer is business economics: as Mr. Sun acknowledges, labor costs in China have been rising rapidly, and there is the lure of large, underserved foreign markets like Nigeria, where competitors are fewer and margins are higher. But another, less obvious answer to this question is that these Chinese entrepreneurs move because they grew up in factories whose bosses had moved to China, and those bosses in turn had grown up in factories with foreign bosses. In short, manufacturing is an industry in which everyone moves to make their next buck.

This point hit home most vividly at a lunch I attended in Maseru, the capital of Lesotho. In the winding hills in a corner of the city, the Avani Lesotho Hotel, the fanciest in town, perches high in a carefully manicured landscape. It was Friday afternoon, and I had spent a long week walking through hot and crowded factories. The blast of the air conditioner as I entered the elegant hotel was a welcome shock.

I was shown downstairs to the Chinese restaurant and into a private dining room—the customary setting in Chinese fine dining. The host of the lunch was already there, perched incongruously in gym shorts and a T-shirt against an elegant dark wood side table. The large round dining table was made of matching wood, and orchids sat on the side tables. Over the next ten minutes, the other guests arrived, a succession of five middle-aged Chinese men. They all knew one another from having been among the only Chinese in Lesotho for much of their working lives, but each politely introduced himself to me. None of them were related, but by sheer coincidence, they were all named Chen.

Lunch commenced in grand fashion. There were oysters on the half shell and salmon sashimi, freshly trucked in from the sea. There was a platter of duck tongues—delicacies in Chinese cuisine—and a half dozen other, more prosaic meats. Soup was served in individual ceramic bowls with matching Chinese-style fat ceramic spoons. As dictated by Chinese custom, red wine was poured into thumb-size glasses for toasting. I had rarely had such an elegant meal in either China or the United States, yet none of the Mr. Chens seemed to share my astonishment.

Despite the lavishness of the setting, the Mr. Chens are not modern-day Chinese versions of the old European colonialists living a life of luxury in Africa. Their backstories show them to be more familiar with "eating bitter"—the Chinese term for working hard—than with eating delicacies. The Mr. Chens all started at the bottom, finding their way from China to Taiwan in the late 1980s and 1990s as hired help. At that time, labor agencies commonly picked up young Chinese workers and matched them with Taiwanese firms in need of cheap labor, and each of the Mr. Chens just happened to be paired with bosses with businesses in Lesotho. Although they had no experience living outside China and Taiwan and no knowledge of English or Sesotho (the local language), each was packed off to the remote African country. Two of the Mr. Chens were extra unlucky: their destination was not the capital city Maseru, but distant mountain villages in the countryside. This being the 1990s, there were no cell phones and no internet. They could call home once a year. As one Mr. Chen reminisced, laughter and bitterness mixed in his voice in equal measure: "That damned phone! I would dial the number, listen for a voice, say something, and wait because there was a delay in transmitting the sound. As soon as I would hear 'Happy new year! How are you?' the line would drop." He shook his head. "In those days, I never had enough money to make a proper phone call home."

After years of hard living and scrimping to save, the Mr. Chens had enough to start their own small businesses. Some started factories, and others ran small shops. A Chinese friend of theirs from that same cohort had cofounded the hotel we were eating in, which explained the careful attention to the niceties of Chinese fine dining. The only man at that lunch not named Mr. Chen was the one who had invited me, and his story was slightly different. Instead of working for Taiwanese bosses in his youth, he had started off working for Japanese companies. "I am still the best Japanese speaker in the entire country of Lesotho!" he boasted after a few rounds of red wine toasts.

The men at that table are the latest link in the historically multinational chain of manufacturing. In academic circles, this phenomenon has been codified as the *flying geese theory*—a mid-20th-century Japanese idea explaining the country's meteoric economic rise. The theory was recently resurrected by the Chinese economist Justin Yifu Lin, the only citizen of a developing country ever to have held the post of chief economist at the World Bank. Studying the success of East Asian countries that rapidly industrialized in the twentieth century the theory postulates that manufacturing firms act like flying geese, migrating from country to country and from product to product as costs and demand change.

The flying geese theory describes the path of the Mr. Chens in Lesotho and Mr. Sun in Nigeria. Without intending to, the long years the Mr. Chens worked for Taiwanese bosses also served as apprenticeships that prepared them to one day run their own enterprises. A wave of Japanese entrepreneurs spawned a wave of Taiwanese entrepreneurs who spawned a wave of Chinese ones. Drawn on a graph of competitiveness over time, the waves form a series of inverted V's, the pattern in which migrating geese fly (figure 1.1). The fact that these Chinese entrepreneurs are now running factories in Africa gives rise to the possibility that the next wave may very well be African.

The flying geese theory has a second dimension: the V's describe not only the movement of manufacturers from country to country, but also a process of industrial upgrading from product to product within each country. According to the theory, first a few firms will show up to try their hand at making a certain product. As they learn, their profits will attract other companies that also try to manufacture that product. But as the field becomes crowded, intensifying competition and thinning profits, some firms will look for a different product. Over time, they'll be pushed to try something slightly more complicated, something that's harder for others to copy. The process will then repeat itself, and countries that started out by copying and learning end up inventing and teaching a mere generation or two later. Mr. Sun's move from leather processing to the more technologically advanced ceramics production is one example of this norm. Remarkably, large-scale, real-world data reveals these inverted V's exactly: an analysis of 148 countries shows that as GDP rises, manufacturers within each country predictably move toward making ever more complicated

FIGURE 1.1 FLYING GEESE IN THEORY
A stylized representation of industrial development

Country: Japan's succession to more technologically advanced products

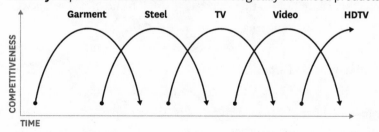

Industry: Garment manufacturing migrates from country to country as product costs and demands change

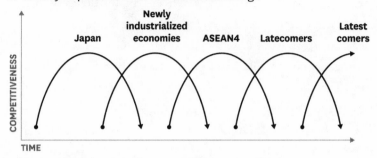

Newly industrialized economies: Hong Kong, Singapore, South Korea, Taiwan
ASEAN4: Indonesia, Malaysia, the Philippines, Thailand
Latecomers: Lesotho, Vietnam, others
Latest comers: Bangladesh, Ethiopia, others

SOURCE: Adapted from Justin Yifu Lin, "From Flying Geese to Leading Dragons: New Opportunities and Strategies for Structural Transformation in Developing Countries," Policy Research Working Paper 5702, Washington, DC, © World Bank 2011

products.[10] Leather yesterday, ceramics today—in another decade or two, Mr. Sun may yet be making computers.

. . .

The flying geese theory is not only a theory about manufacturing, but also about how development happens—and what it means. Development is not just about a lucky few getting fabulously rich; it's about ordinary people experiencing lives that are easier and more comfortable in a thousand small ways. As such, it affects not only people directly involved in factories, but all the rest of us as well.

I was born in Changchun, a provincial capital of two million people in Manchuria, the vast swath of China that lies between Russia and North Korea. In the late 1980s, my father left for a year to take a postdoctoral fellowship in Japan, leaving my mother and two-year-old me with his family in China. I was too young to remember when he left, but I do remember when he returned, because he brought back a marvel: plastic wrap.

In the China of the 1980s, no one had a refrigerator, very few had a television, and soft drinks like Coke and Sprite were expensive treats my parents meted out when I really behaved myself. Meat was still rationed through state-issued coupons, and less than a generation from the mass starvation of the Great Leap Forward, it was unacceptable to let food go to waste. But flies in the summer and the dryness of coal-fired central heating in the winter quickly made any leftovers unappetizing. I, like everyone else in my family, had to eat them nonetheless. This was a real burden on my three-year-old self.

Enter my father with the plastic wrap. He brought back a whole suitcase of it from Japan. He took out one box and showed us how to glide a finger along the roll to find the edge, how to cut a sheet on the serrated blade, and how to stretch it over a bowl without having it clump together. It was magic. At that time, China, with more than a fifth of the world's population, accounted for only 3 percent of global manufacturing output, and no one in my family had ever seen anything like it.[11] I wasn't allowed to touch the precious, glimmering film brought from afar. Nonetheless, it made my life better, because it made leftovers much more palatable. My parents divided the contents of the suitcase between our family's use and gifts for friends and higher-ups at work. At that time, giving gifts from abroad was a sign of good taste, and anyone to whom my parents gave a roll of the precious plastic wrap implicitly owed us a favor afterward.

What I didn't realize at the time was that the reason Japan had plastic wrap and China did not was because Japan had factories, whereas China did not. At the beginning of what economists would eventually term "the East Asian miracle," Japan became the first industrialized country in East Asia.[12] In so doing, it set a record for the fastest sustained rise in living standards that any country had achieved in the history of the world, crushing the time it had taken the United States (sixty years) and the United Kingdom (fifty years) to reach industrialized status. Then Japanese firms relocating abroad helped catalyze record-breaking economic growth in other countries. This next wave—in the Four Asian Tigers of Hong Kong, Singapore, South Korea, and Taiwan—in turn beat Japan's record for rapid economic growth. Whereas Japan had taken thirty-five years to double its GDP, South Korea took only eleven and became the first country to rise from the UN's "least developed country" status to membership in the Organisation for Economic Co-operation and Development (OECD), the club of wealthy nations.[13]

It was no accident, then, that these same countries invested in factories in China. As Mr. Sun was dropping out of school and going to work in a factory in Wenzhou, foreign investment from companies experiencing high costs in their home countries flooded into China, and large numbers of Chinese laborers, like the Mr. Chens, went to work for Taiwanese and other foreign firms. In the early 1980s, when China was poorer on a per cap-ita basis than Ethiopia and Mali, Deng Xiaoping set the country a target that seemed crazy at the time: quadrupling its GDP in twenty years and quadrupling it again in another fifty years—that is, increasing it sixteenfold by 2050.[14] Ignoring the Washington Consensus and other Western development advice, the Chinese strategy was Mr. Sun's strategy on a grand scale: learn how to make things, make them, and sell them.

It worked. China became the Factory of the World, accounting for a quarter of the entire global manufacturing output.[15] In the process, its GDP grew at nearly 10 percent a year for three decades, lifting 750 million people out of poverty—the most that any nation has ever accomplished.[16] China beat South Korea's record for doubling GDP, doing it in only nine years and erasing any suspicion that the flying geese theory applied only to the small countries of Asia. And as for Deng's target? It did turn out to be crazy, but crazy *low*: instead of seventy years, it took China sixteen years to grow its GDP sixteenfold.[17]

Needless to say, plastic wrap is no longer a foreign novelty in China. That's not because more people became educated like my dad and were able to bring it back from developed countries. Nor is it because Chinese people got rich and could then buy plastic wrap. Instead, it was the other way around: they made plastic wrap and got rich as a result. China makes a quarter of all the plastics in the world today, and not coincidentally, ordinary people can now afford plastic wrap. As Mr. Sun's and the Mr. Chens' stories show, the best way to get what you want may very well be to make it yourself.

CHAPTER 2

The Life, Death, and Rebirth of Factories

When Lawrence Tung met me at the reception desk, I thought he was an assistant or maybe the receptionist who had stepped away for a moment, not the boss himself. His slight frame was engulfed in an oversize Abercrombie polo shirt and a pair of baggy, dark-gray jeans. He led me to his office, showed me to a seat, and took his place behind a massive wraparound desk. His thick black hair was overgrown and stuck out perpendicularly from his scalp. As he settled in behind the desk, he called to mind nothing so much as a teenager in his father's office.

Despite his youthful appearance, Lawrence is actually the executive director and third-generation owner of Wempco, one of the largest privately held firms in Nigeria. His family came to Nigeria fifty years ago from China via Hong Kong. Their factories churn out wood products, smelted and rolled steel, and ceramics. The family sends its kids to be educated in Hong Kong and the United States—Lawrence is a Wharton grad—but by and large, they live and work in Nigeria. A few years ago, Lawrence even renounced

US citizenship in favor of Nigerian citizenship. As he explained, "We're here for the long run. This is our second home."

Lawrence's family history is a reminder that now is not the first time Chinese industrialists have landed in Africa.* Nor is it the first time Africa looked like it might industrialize.[1] There's nothing easy about the process, and it's not a sure thing today, just as it wasn't fifty years ago. When the Tungs and other eager Chinese industrialists showed up in the 1960s, Africa seemed poised for take-off, with government policies emphasizing industrial sectors, a small but promising industrial base left behind by European colonizers, and a general sense of optimism from being newly independent. But the following years brought devastating shocks: a macroeconomic crisis, worsening government corruption and ineptitude, and increasingly fierce global competition. In Nigeria, two of the four big Chinese family-run industrial firms collapsed. As a whole, Nigeria—and the rest of Africa—deindustrialized.

But the lessons of history run both ways at once. Even in the face of headwinds, there is often a way to do business. The remaining two family-run firms not only survived, but thrived. Macroeconomic conditions have been better in the past fifteen years than in previous decades across many parts of Africa, and that has attracted hundreds of new Chinese manufacturing investments. The Tungs and other old-timers know that conditions are always temporary, that another downturn could come any time, yet they are confident in their ability to do business in Africa for

---

*In fact, historians would point out that the Tungs' arrival in the mid twentieth century was actually the third wave of Chinese immigration to Africa. The first wave came in the form of prisoners brought by the Dutch via Southeast Asia in the seventeenth century. The second wave consisted of Chinese contract laborers who came to the continent during the height of European colonialism, in the late nineteenth and early twentieth centuries. For example, in 1904, the British government brought 64,000 Chinese indentured laborers to work in South African gold mines.

generations to come. Macroeconomics is important, but it is not destiny. The decisions of companies and individuals still matter, and sometimes they make the difference between adversity that kills a business and adversity that sharpens it into the best in the world.

The best in the world—in Africa. This is not an exaggerated ambition, and despite the history of the past fifty years, during which Nigeria seemed to thwart its own chances for industrialization, it doesn't seem far-fetched to Lawrence. In the middle of our conversation, he described how his family has branched out in recent years into the hospitality business. While factories are still the heart of their enterprise, they've opened a luxury hotel in Lagos, Nigeria's largest city. "The brief that we gave the chef at our hotel was to create a three-star Michelin restaurant," Lawrence said. "Obviously there's nothing like that today in Nigeria, so it's very difficult." Yet he looked unfazed. "We have been here for fifty years and aren't bleeding money. We can wait another fifty years."

. . .

Factories live and die. They take root in a place, thrive for a while, and then fade away. From British textile factories in the nineteenth century to Detroit auto plants and Japanese TV makers in the twentieth, factories come, then factories go.

In Africa in the 1960s and 1970s, factories were coming to life. In the heady years following independence from European colonialism for vast swaths of the continent, both foreign investors and national governments were optimistic about the prospects for large-scale manufacturing in Africa. Shortly after Nigeria's independence from Great Britain, in 1960, foreign investment helped create the first textile mill in the country. Kaduna Textile Mills was an immediate success, turning a profit from its very first month in operation.[2] A former manager recounts how by just taking around samples of his product, "a fabric heavily filled with starch and cal-endered so that it almost shone," he was "able to sell six months' production within a morning's stroll around Manchester and a brief visit to Liverpool, with only the inconvenience of taking one of the buyers out to lunch."[3] More companies entered the market, looking for a piece of the action, and Nigeria soon became a major textiles production hub.

Today the Nigerian economy is almost synonymous with oil, but there was a time when the Nigeria's largest sector was that most classic of manufactured products: textiles. The cloth pro-duced in Nigeria's factories was prized not only within its own borders, and not only in West Africa, but also in such sophisticated markets as Great Britain. By the early 1970s, Nigeria was produc-ing half the cotton cloth in all of West Africa. Continent-wide, its textile industry was second only to Egypt's in size.

In the late 1980s, the Nigerian textile industry encompassed two hundred firms and was the second-largest employer after the government.[4] Beyond factory jobs, there were jobs for the growers who supplied the raw cotton, the ginners who did the initial processing, the parts suppliers who provided machinery components, and the distributors who sold the finished cloth. At its height, the industry directly employed a million workers and was also indirectly responsible for several million other jobs along this value chain.[5]

In those early years of Nigeria's manufacturing sector, Chinese investment was already showing up. Lawrence Tung's predeces-sors were part of that wave of migration, and one of what the Chinese community in Nigeria reverently refer to as the Four Great Families. These were industrialist families who had fled to Hong Kong after the Communist takeover of China in 1949. But business in Hong Kong was tough, because many other capitalists fleeing China had landed there with the same idea. Consequently, numerous companies started looking to relocate abroad, and a few showed up in Africa. The Four Great Families were the most successful of these migrants in Nigeria; they became manufacturing moguls in their adopted home. Two of the four made the product du jour: textiles. In fact, the largest business in the entire country was once United Nigeria Textiles, which was Chinese-owned. At its height in the 1980s, it employed more than 20,000 people and was the biggest textile factory in all of Africa.[6]

United Nigeria Textiles still exists, but it no longer manufactures anything in Nigeria. By 2010, Nigeria's once glorious textile industry was down to one-tenth of its former size, with only twenty-four firms left.[7] Even the venerable Kaduna Textile Mills, which had started it all, shut down in the mid-2000s.[8] The remaining companies stumbled along using decades-old technology at an average of 20 percent capacity utilization.[9] Laborers and even the textile workers union agreed to pay cuts, but firm after firm shut down and laid off its workers. By the late 2000s, industrywide employment had shrunk to 18,000 people, fewer than the figure United Nigeria Textiles alone had employed two decades earlier.[10] Three million workers' jobs vanished.[11] Entire communities were devastated. Two scholars who studied the industry described the "dejection" and "chronic poverty" that set in when the mills closed, as former employees made do with informal work, were forced into crime, or even met early deaths.[12]

What happened to Nigeria's textile industry? The decline of this once dominant sector defies simple explanation and is the result of the interplay between three macroeconomic forces: the "resource curse," shortsighted government policies, and global competition.

The paradoxical-sounding "resource curse" refers to the phenomenon whereby a windfall in natural resource discoveries ironically results in a country's becoming poorer, not richer. In 1957, Shell and BP discovered oil in the Niger Delta region, setting off a mad rush of investment. By the early 1970s, oil money was flooding into the country. A sharp upward demand for local currency caused the Nigerian naira to appreciate significantly against global currencies. That encouraged textile manufacturers to import all the equipment, raw materials, and spare parts they needed rather than develop suppliers domestically.[13]

The appreciating naira also subjected Nigeria's manufacturing sector to "Dutch disease." Named for the unlucky Dutch who first experienced its effects in the 1950s after discovering natural gas, Dutch disease cripples an economy by making non-resources sectors uncompetitive. Because oil was so lucrative in Nigeria, investment shifted from manufacturing into resource extraction. The more the naira appreciated against global currencies, the more expensive Nigeria's manufactured goods became for the rest of the world. Depending on the industry, this effect may be counterbalanced by relatively lower input prices. For a while, this worked for Nigeria's textile industry, which became artificially profitable because its imported inputs could be purchased with fewer naira. But even that was a double-edged sword, because its finished goods were still increasingly expensive for the rest of the world—so Nigeria's non-oil exports plummeted. As their products became less affordable, Nigerian textile producers went from being strong exporters to serving only the domestic market. As late as 1970, more than 40 percent of Nigeria's exports were non-oil, but that figure had dropped below 20 percent by 1973 and below 10 percent by the 1990s.[14] Into the 1980s, the industry looked profitable, but the strong naira had caused it to become dangerously unbalanced: it was buying all its inputs and machinery from abroad while selling all its output domestically.

Then the real trouble hit. In the early 1980s, oil prices collapsed globally. Nigeria, whose economy had become dangerously dependent on oil exports, faced galloping inflation, increasing unemployment, and a balance-of-payments crisis. Government debt ballooned from less than 10 percent of GDP in 1980 to more than 100 percent of GDP a mere six years later. In 1986, with no other options left, Nigeria accepted the IMF's Structural Adjustment Program, a package of emergency loans that gave it a much-needed fiscal lifeline in exchange for acceptance of Washington Consensus policies of privatization and liberalization of the economy. A main thrust was the adoption of a floating exchange rate program with no predefined rates of change. From an exchange rate of roughly 2 naira to US$1 at the beginning of the program, the naira depreciated to 4 in 1987, to 10 in 1991, and further to 22 in 1998.[15] By the time I met Lawrence Tung, in 2013, the rate was 165 naira to the dollar.

For textile mills, the continued drop in the currency's value was devastating, because they could no longer afford to import needed spare parts and machinery, and decades of importing them meant that no domestic suppliers existed to fill those needs. As a result, the industry's productivity fell faster and faster. In the mid-1980s, a World Bank study found that 70,000 of the industry's spindles were "technologically obsolete" and that its active machinery was performing at 30 percent below its rated level of efficiency.[16] At the same time, the collapsing naira meant that customers—all domestic—could no longer afford the mills' products, and former foreign customers, now accustomed to buying from other countries, could not be recovered in the near term.

Added to this dismal spate of macroeconomic misfortune was hapless government policy. In the face of the textile industry's many troubles, the Nigerian government sought to shield domestic industries from foreign competition by enacting high tariffs. The import duty on woven cotton fabric went from 20 percent in 1957—fairly low for its time—to 50 percent a decade later, and was again raised for some types of fabric and clothing to 80–136 percent by 1971.[17] With these tariffs in place, Nigerian textile mills felt less and less pressure to be globally competitive, because they could be increasingly inefficient compared with their foreign competitors and still enjoy a profit.

To be fair, such a policy—which is called import substitution industrialization—was popular around the world at that time. The thinking was that if the government could protect domestic producers from foreign competition for a while, the producers would get better at what they did, become competitive against firms abroad, and eventually substitute domestic production for goods that had previously been imported. Unfortunately, the more the Nigerian government tried to give preference to domestic production over imports, the worse the problem became. Protectionism merely prolonged the decline of inefficient firms but did not raise productivity and therefore failed to prevent their ultimate death. Even as the government continued to raise tariffs, the domestic textile industry continued to shrink.

Furthermore, the Nigerian government did its textile industry no favors in other policy realms. It neglected infrastructure maintenance and investment, making it painful for companies to obtain power—an irony given Nigeria's newfound dominance in the global energy market. As one textile worker explained to scholars years later, "When I started in Kaduna Textiles . . . you would be proud to call yourself a textile worker . . . [One] government policy that affected the textile industry, power, is not steady. When I started it was perfect . . . The issue of black oil, its cost shot up by 400 per cent or more."[18] Owing to years of government neglect, the power grid in Nigeria was highly unreliable, forcing textile firms to rely on backup generators and expensive low pour fuel oil, commonly termed black oil.

The Nigerian government's deteriorating efficacy and the resource curse were mutually reinforcing: each fed into the other through the creation of a rentier state. Instead of acting as a manager and a steward of national resources, the Nigerian government increasingly leeched from them. As the Brookings Institute noted, "Political pressures which would have improved the taxation of personal incomes, farm incomes, or property incomes were absent because everyone believed that oil revenue will always lead to surplus."[19] This unhealthy shrinking of the tax base to little more than oil receipts reduced the government's obligation to provide reliable services, as the existence of taxpayers has the salutatory benefit of putting pressure on the government to provide services in exchange for those taxes. Absent such accountability, the Nigerian government shirked ever more responsibility for infrastructure, public services, and routine administration, and some government officials even engaged in outright theft. In 2012, a former World Bank vice president for Africa estimated that $400 billion worth of Nigeria's oil revenues had been stolen or misspent since independence in 1960.[20]

But in addition to what the Nigerians did or did not do, the textile industry's death was also precipitated by what non-Nigerians learned to do. That is to say, during this period, Asian firms figured out how to make cloth more efficiently than the rest of the world could. With the help of foreign investment and favorable national policies, East Asian textile production shot up astronomically. For example, from 1968 to 1973, South Korean textile and clothing output grew by an average of 26 percent a year, and exports grew by an astonishing 47 percent a year.[21] South Korea is emblematic in this regard: since the 1970s, manufacturing value addition has grown by an average of 8–10 percent a year across China, Hong Kong, Indonesia, Malaysia, the Philippines, Singapore, South Korea, Taiwan, and Thailand.[22] The story is dramatic: as sub-Saharan Africa's share of global textile manufacturing dropped from 1.9 percent in the 1970s to 0.1 percent in the early 2000s, Asian developing countries' share rose from 8 percent to 25 percent.[23] As Nigeria became dangerously enamored with oil, Asia became the textile production center of the world.

These three developments—a domestic industry plagued by macroeconomic shocks, a corrupt and inept national government, and foreign competitors that learned to make products cheaply and efficiently—combined to create conditions ripe for an insidious development: smuggling. In 1977, desperate to revive the already struggling industry, the Nigerian government replaced the tariff system with an outright ban on textile imports. But the price differential between Asian and Nigerian textiles was already so high that smugglers could ship in the cheaper Asian textiles, pay off customs officials, sell at a lower price than what domestic firms could afford to produce at, and still make a handsome profit. Hence the import ban had exactly the opposite of its intended effect: rather than resuscitating a dying textile industry, it created the perfect set of incentives for smuggling and thus provided the final death sentence for domestic industry.[24] What's more, tariff revenues also disappeared: what had previously been government income from import duties now lined the pockets of corrupt customs officials instead.

Much of the smuggled textiles and clothing that poured into Nigeria came from China. As a result, Nigerians commonly blame China for the demise of their textile industry in particular and of their manufacturing sector more generally. As one major Nigerian daily newspaper put it, "The textile industry today is faced with many problems but the major problem and concern is the smuggling of fabrics, which remain uncontrolled. This smuggling is characterised by copying of our designs and trademarks, printed in the Asian countries and brought into Nigerian markets."[25] It didn't help that the Chinatown in Lagos appeared to be a major smuggling hub. In February 2006, the Nigerian Customs Department discovered thirty trailer-loads of contraband textiles and clothing there. In response, the comptroller-general shut down Chinatown and arrested several Chinese businessmen, citing "flagrant abuse and violations of Nigeria's economic and fiscal policies by the Chinese."[26] Within a few days, in an unusual move, the Nigerian Senate took jurisdiction over the matter; it quickly released the businessmen and allowed Chinatown to reopen for business, fueling suspicions of backroom dealings and bribery. It turns out there is no national allegiance when it comes to making money. First Chinese industrialists helped create the Nigerian textile industry, then Chinese smugglers helped kill it.

This same ill-fated combination of macroeconomic shifts, policy-making ineptitude, and rising global competition was killing other parts of Nigeria's manufacturing sector as well. Although manufacturing represented a respectable 10 percent of its national GDP in 1960, the share was down to 2 percent by 2010.[27] Proportionately, that's a greater drop than what the state of Michigan experienced during the same period, when Detroit tumbled from auto capital of the world to America's preeminent example of urban blight.

To be sure, Nigeria's manufacturing sector has had a particularly precipitous decline, but it is emblematic of trends across the continent.[28] Ghana's manufacturing sector as a share of total GDP declined by half from 1960 to 2010, and Tanzania's declined by a third. Overall, African nations had more robust manufacturing sectors in the years immediately following independence from colonialism in the 1960s and the 1970s than they have today. Manufacturing now accounts for only 13 percent of Africa's GDP and 25 percent of its exports, both smaller shares than in any other region of the world save the oil-rich Middle East.[29] Far from becoming industrial powerhouses in which large-scale factories might be expected to flourish, African countries have deindustrialized over the past half century. In the grand view of the life and death of factories, Africa's enjoyed but a brief life.

. . .

And yet today, African factories are experiencing a rebirth. This is curious: as with Britain's textile firms two centuries ago or Detroit's auto plants today, once factories start dying, they normally don't revive. As we have seen, Africa's factories, never very robust to begin with, seemed to have died out in the 1980s and

1990s. But like a phoenix rising from the ashes, factories such as those of the Tung family are more competitive, and their owners more confident, than ever. Three years ago, the Tungs made a huge investment in Africa's largest cold-rolled-steel plant: a $1.5 billion bet on the economy of Nigeria and their company's ability to do business there for the long term.[30] The other Great Family that survived the lean times is expanding as well: the Lee Group has built new factories in Nigeria to produce everything from plastic bags to bread and bottled water. These longtime Chinese investors are now reinvesting heavily, while new Chinese entrepreneurs are showing up on African shores in ever-larger numbers each year. If a first wave of Chinese industrialists helped give life to African manufacturing, then a wave of Chinese smugglers helped kill it, now a new wave of Chinese investment is bringing it back to life.

Until recently, little data had been collected about Chinese investment in Africa. I co-led a large-scale research project at McKinsey & Company, the global management consulting firm, to change this state of affairs. We hired a small army of Chinese freelance journalists, PhD students, and former employees of state-owned enterprises, trained them to conduct an hour-long survey, and sent them out to network their way into Chinese communities in eight major African countries representing three-quarters of sub-Saharan African GDP. We discovered more than ten thousand Chinese firms—a degree of activity and confidence in doing business in Africa that no one expected.[31] In the eight countries where we did fieldwork, we found nearly four times as many Chinese firms as there were in the previous largest database. One-third— about 1,500—of the Chinese businesses in these eight countries were manufacturers. If this proportion holds continent-wide, there are already three to four thousand Chinese manufacturers in Africa.

Skeptics may point out that the large number of companies may not matter if they tend to be small. But although Chinese manufacturing investments tend to be smaller than the large-scale infrastructure projects that dominate the news about China's presence in Africa, those factories are not puny. We surveyed nearly 200 manufacturing firms, and their average annual revenues was $21 million—far exceeding the cutoff defining small and medium enterprises in most African countries. And nearly all those firms are privately owned as opposed to being Chinese state-owned enterprises (SOEs), suggesting that these investments are driven by profit motives rather than by government directives. This may surprise readers familiar with reports that emphasize links between the Chinese government and Chinese business in Africa. But China is a vast place, and large sections of the economy are privately run. After all, most factory bosses in China work for themselves. As Yang Wenyi, a Chinese investor in multiple manufacturing plants in Nigeria, told me, "I have no use for the government. I'm not doing anything illegal, and I'm not looking for government contracts."[32] Private entrepreneurs making tangible goods for private sector consumers: this is how Chinese manufacturing firms work, in Africa as they do in China.

To be clear, this level of manufacturing investment in Africa by a foreign player is unique. By contrast, the $14 billion of US private sector investment in Africa announced by the Obama administration in August 2014 focuses primarily on banking, construction, and information technology.[33] That is for good reason: after decades of relocating their factories to developing countries, the United States and other developed nations have very little manufacturing left to offshore. In Europe, Japan, and North America, the manufacturing share of employment has steadily declined from the 20–40 percent range in 1970 to half that figure in 2012.[34] Other than China, most developing countries never had that much to begin with: Brazil's peak in share of manufacturing employment was 16 percent in 1986; India hit its peak at just

13 percent, in 2002.[35] Only China has enough of a manufacturing sector left to offshore, and much of that appears to be moving to Africa.

. . .

But how could this be? Why would manufacturing in Africa, an industry that by all measures died a generation ago, be attracting so much investment today?

There are two answers to this question: a structural one, and an individual one. The structural answer takes a macroeconomic view of the large-scale changes taking place in the global economy. Robert Lawrence, a Harvard economist and South African by birth, puts it this way: "Globally, as major countries like China move out of the bottom of the economic ladder, there is a major opportunity for those countries still remaining at the bottom."[36] It turns out that being at the bottom has its benefits—what economists have long identified as "the advantages of economic backwardness."[37] First, low-income countries are just that—low-income, with wage rates cheaper than those of richer countries, making them attractive destinations for industries with high labor needs. Second, because most poor countries still have the lion's share of their economic output and employment in relatively low-productivity types of agriculture, they have ample scope for productivity increases. That is to say, it's not hard to show growth when one is starting from a low base. And third, instead of costly trial and error in developing high-productivity technologies, latecomer developing countries can adopt tried-and-true technologies and innovations from earlier, pathbreaking countries.[38] As Asian countries get rich, copying the machines and production methods they pioneered provides an opportunistic catch-up strategy for African countries that have yet to industrialize.

This logic—predicated upon how far African nations have fallen behind global wage and productivity levels—is admittedly unflattering to Africa, but it's a solid structural explanation as to why the flying geese are flocking to Africa now. And it's backed up by the entrepreneurs themselves: in my research, I have met dozens of Chinese factory owners who cite rising labor costs in China and the ability to import technology as primary reasons for doing business in Africa.

Yet this doesn't explain why Lawrence Tung's family is willing to stay in Nigeria for another fifty years, come whatever macro-economic conditions may. What's more, they're doubling down, not only maintaining their existing factories, but also betting big on a $1.5 billion steel plant whose opening ceremony was attended by the Nigerian president.[39] How is it that they who have suffered the worst—an oil crisis, a military dictatorship, a national bailout by the IMF, an exchange rate that dropped like a stone—remain so optimistic about manufacturing in Nigeria?

Here is where the individual answer matters. Structural forces are suggestive, but not decisive. Personal commitment and company-level ingenuity still count. That's not to say that structural explanations aren't valid, but instead to acknowledge that even the best of conditions require individuals willing to bet their livelihoods that they can make it work. Progress results when individuals meet a context, act to change it, and are changed in the process.

. . .

Neon pink. Creamy white. Camouflage green. Tangerine orange. Gently steaming, sheets of light, foamy rubber come off the machine like extra-large, improbably colored sheets of cookie dough. Workers take them to racks to cool. They pause to double-check their instructions, stacking sheets in prescribed color combinations: navy-cream-navy, black-white-vermillion. The stacked sheets go first into a machine that compresses them together and then into another machine that stamps foot-shaped cuts into the

45

sheets. Workers punch out the feet, careful to keep them in batches according to style and size. The foot shapes go on a conveyor belt, and other workers remove them to attach Y-shaped straps. Multi-colored nubs of foam—the bits of shoe bed punched out where the strap attaches to the sole—dot the floor like confetti. One worker goes around sweeping them up to be mixed back into a future batch of colored rubber, for yet more flip-flops.

It is difficult to identify the highest-volume shoe factory in the world, since no organization I know of keeps statistics to that effect. But more likely than not, this is it: a flip-flop factory in Nigeria owned by the Lees, the other of the Four Great Families whose business remains intact. In addition to manufacturing bottled water, bread, plastic bags, and steel, the Lee Group produces 1.2 million pairs of flip-flops *a day*. This single firm makes more than enough flip-flops for every man, woman, and child in the United States—or two pairs for every man, woman, and child in Nigeria—each year.

There is no better proof that Africa can industrialize than the humming of this factory, owned by people who survived the worst and came out of it believing even more in the promise of African manufacturing. They believe in it not because they think conditions will always be favorable, but because they are confident in their own ability to find the right business model for those conditions. As the manager who gave me the factory tour explained, the whole reason for his company's success is that the Lee Group decided to do precisely the opposite of what its competitors do. Flip-flop factories in China are comparatively smaller and more flexibly constructed so that they can make a different range of styles with each new season. But most Nigerian consumers prefer low prices over new styles, so the Lee Group produces very few styles, but in much larger volumes. They achieve higher efficiency through standardization: they do little except change the colors on their best-selling item, a basic flip-flop that retails for about a dollar a pair. As a result, they can run this large-scale factory almost continuously, resulting in lower per-unit costs than flip-flop factories in China can achieve.

Although the Lee Group has a "99.99 percent market share" in Nigeria and its surrounding countries, it doesn't use this monopoly power to raise prices. The company understands that its business model relies on consumers who are unwilling or unable to afford more, so it continues to sell its flip-flops at a price no smuggler can possibly match. It found just the right business model to turn an unfavorable contextual factor—poor, price-sensitive consumers— into a gold mine. As a result, there are no smuggled flip-flops in Nigeria. This is how the company has stayed in business for half a century while many other manufacturers floundered.

Owing to this world-class cost structure and disciplined pricing policy, the Lee Group's flip-flop business is thriving. A couple of years ago, it was paid the ultimate compliment when Walmart, the world's largest retailer, came calling. Walmart wanted to know whether the Lee Group would consider becoming its flip-flop supplier. The Lee Group said no. The company has long sold all its flip-flops at its factory gates to local wholesalers, who take the shoes to every corner of Nigeria and into surrounding countries in West Africa. It has never had any trouble selling its entire output and didn't see the point of disappointing long-standing distributors in order to serve Walmart. It didn't need the business of the largest retailer in the world because it had found a more efficient production model to serve an even more price-conscious consumer. In some sense, it had outWalmarted Walmart.

CHAPTER 3

Cloth and Clothing, Steel Rods and Steel Sheets

Half a continent away, in the tiny mountain kingdom of Lesotho, Mrs. Shen is having a bad day. Her husband is sitting in the air-conditioned office of their factory, pretending to work but in reality just whiling the hours away on his smartphone. Meanwhile, Mrs. Shen has been working nonstop on the factory floor, which has no air-conditioning and is hot from absorbing the southern African summer sun through its metal roof.

The only reason Mrs. Shen softens toward me is that my mother is from Shanghai, which is her hometown as well. Upon learning this, Mrs. Shen switches from her somewhat stilted Mandarin to a rapid stream of Shanghai dialect. I have to explain apologetically that because my dad is a northerner, I never learned to speak Shanghainese. Mrs. Shen looks annoyed again, so I quickly mention that my mom's surname also happens to be Shen. This makes me acceptable once more, and she agrees to show me around the factory.

As we step into the main room, the decibel level jumps several notches. The low-ceilinged room reverberates with sharp bursts of sewing from hundreds of closely packed machines. Scraps of cloth litter the floor. Workers sit in rows, each one behind a sewing machine. Each row forms a production line that is responsible for sewing pieces of fabric together in just the right way to make a Reebok workout T-shirt. Within each line, workers pass batches of work-in-progress clothing to one another, sewing one more seam or adding one more component as they go. Mrs. Shen is fretting that production for this Reebok order is falling slightly behind, and since her English is rudimentary, she has trouble instructing her employees how to work faster. But she is constantly monitoring the ten production lines on the floor, and when she notices that one is lagging behind or another is waiting for work, she makes adjustments, load-balancing the batches so that everyone has something to do all the time. (Later on, in part two, we'll look at the situation from the perspective of Lesotho garment workers dealing with Chinese bosses.) Mrs. Shen sighs that these solid athletic T-shirts look simple but are actually complicated to make: they involve no fewer than four plastic heat-appliquéd markers that have to be individually aligned by hand and stamped into place using a specialized machine. She motions me into a side room, and sure enough, it's full of workers busily Reebok-ing every shirt four times. The machines let out a hiss as they stamp each tiny trademark triangle into place.[1]

Mrs. Shen and the other Chinese factory owners in Lesotho's clothing industry know nothing about the death of the textile industry a generation ago in Nigeria—nor should they. But they nonetheless present a curious contrast with Nigeria's textile mills. Why is Mrs. Shen's Lesotho factory thriving by manufacturing Reebok T-shirts for American consumers, when United Nigeria Textiles couldn't survive making cloth for Nigerians? If the past generation of factories largely died out, why would this generation be any more likely to bring large-scale industrialization to Africa?

As we shall see, the answer lies in the multiplicity of business models that are included under the blanket heading "manufacturing in Africa." Grand narratives about manufacturing have always been simple stories, whether the old adage that factories tend to locate where labor costs are lowest, or the new one that manufacturing will soon use no labor at all and instead rely entirely on robots. But the real story is more complicated, and more interesting. Whenever I met Chinese entrepreneurs in Africa, I asked them how they came to be doing what they do, where they do. Their stories blew me away with their diversity. Sometimes they had chosen their business because they knew it from previous jobs, or it was what they could afford to invest in. Sometimes they had figured out an ingenious, entirely new business model. Sometimes they had been attracted to the infrastructure or macro conditions of a country, or were driven to a new location by global trade policy made half a world away. The picture is of entrepreneurs doing their best to respond to a complex reality, trying to make their mark—and make some money—in a game in which they have little control over what cards they're dealt.

Rather than being mindless sweatshops taking advantage of cheap labor, African factories today are continually responding to a host of factors, from the macroeconomic to the individual. Their business models have varying effects on workers: some factories employ large numbers of people, others very few; some jobs are likely to stick around through economic downturns, others are much easier to move. Far from affecting all parts of Africa in the same way, growth is uneven, occurring in pockets: as events unfold, changing conditions favor some business models and not others, some countries and not others. This unevenness has a benefit: unlike the relatively uniform lot of textile mills in Nigeria, modern factories in Africa are a varied bunch, making it far less likely that a single macroeconomic event or contextual shock could wipe out the entire sector. In short, diversity is also resiliency.

. . .

Chinese-owned factories in Africa make a wide range of goods, from overstuffed leather couches to delicate gel capsules for drugs, from form-fitting yoga pants for Americans to steel rods for local housing construction. How can we make sense of this disparate list and the various business models it represents? It turns out that this diversity can nonetheless be classified into four groups, each of which represent a different way of doing business, with different types of supply chains involved and different consequences for local job creation. These four categories form at the intersection of two dimensions: how the goods are made, and who the customers are (figure 3.1).

The first dimension is a classic choice in economics between labor-intensive and capital-intensive methods of production. For entrepreneurs, this choice is critical because it determines how much of their money will be held up in the enterprise and how much hands-on management of labor will be required. For an African country hosting Chinese factories, this dimension determines the volume of local job creation and also how likely it is that the factory will remain for a sustained period of time. Although clothing and textiles may appear to be similar products, shutting down a clothing factory is straightforward, whereas calling it quits on a textile mill requires a far more considered decision. With a clothing factory, you simply send your workers home and try to sell your sewing machines. A textile mill involves tens of millions of dollars' worth of highly specialized machinery, making it far more complicated to find buyers and transport the machinery to them.

The other dimension is who the customers are. Are the goods destined for consumers in-country, or will they be exported to foreign markets? This is a major dividing line for factories, because it dictates what demand signals they need to respond to in designing their products and how long and complicated of a supply chain they must understand and manage. It is commonly assumed that

FIGURE 3.1 TWO MAJOR DIMENSIONS
FOR UNDERSTANDING CHINESE FACTORIES IN AFRICA

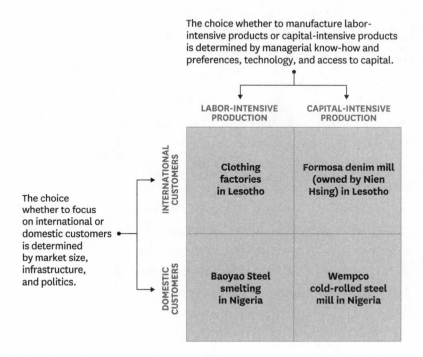

this dimension also determines a factory's competitor set—in particular, how exposed the factory will be to foreign competition. But as we saw in the previous chapter, owing to increased trade and smuggling, even factories that target only the domestic market are competing with products made half a world away. Nigeria's bungling of trade policy illustrates that firms can be powerfully steered in one direction or the other—toward serving primarily domestic consumers or toward exporting globally—by government policy. And if Nigeria's protectionism is at one end of the spectrum, the preferential trade policies enacted over the past few decades by the European Union and the United States are at the other. Clothing firms sought out Lesotho specifically because the EU gave imports from Lesotho tariff-free access to its market under the Lomé Convention; when that expired, the African Growth and Opportunity Act (AGOA) did the same for the US market. In this way, Asian-owned clothing manufacturers were effectively induced to route value chains to serve European and American consumers by way of Africa.

The four categories matter because they have enormous consequences for African countries, from both a job-creation and a risk perspective. Labor-intensive factories employ many people, but their jobs are fleeting in the case of a downturn. Capital-intensive factories may employ fewer people, but their high fixed costs mean that they often continue to operate even when conditions are less favorable, making their jobs "stickier." Factories serving international customers have the benefit of a larger market, but it opens them up to additional risks: exchange rate fluctuations, trade agreements, or even something as simple but decisive as a shift in consumer tastes in a faraway country.

Let's walk through four real factories that illustrate these dynamics. The first is Mrs. Shen's clothing factory. It's one of approximately twenty clothing manufacturers in Lesotho that share the same business model: labor-intensive operations, global customers. These manufacturers fulfill orders for major brands familiar to any American shopper: Levi's, Walmart, Kohl's, and the like. The largest of them employ several thousand workers, and the smallest have a few dozen, just enough for a couple of production lines. Many of the factories on the small end of the spectrum are subcontractors to larger firms that handle the overall customer order and parcel out what they cannot do in-house.

Mrs. Shen's factory, with a few hundred workers, is toward the smaller end of the spectrum. True to type, Mrs. Shen got her start in the clothing business in Lesotho by working as a manager in another, larger clothing factory, where she gained a sense of how the industry works. Slowly, she became confident in her ability to manage a factory of her own. When she saw that there was more work than the factory she was employed by could handle, she decided to take advantage of the opportunity. Using her and her husband's savings, she started her own factory.

Although Mrs. Shen is the boss, her factory does not generate work orders; it simply takes them from other factories, including her previous employer. This means her costs are low: literally the only assets on Mrs. Shen's books are several hundred sewing and stamping machines. Not even the gray and blue cloth that Mrs. Shen's factory uses to make the Reebok T-shirts sits on her balance sheet; it remains on the books of the contracting firm. The only value that factories like Mrs. Shen's add is labor.

This may come as a surprise in an age of automation and widespread unease that robots are poised to replace human laborers. But observe the work that Mrs. Shen's employees do, and it becomes clear why humans are still indispensable to this sort of manufacturing. First the cloth must be cut into specific shapes, in varying sizes corresponding to clothing sizes. Then the bits of cloth must be arranged and sewn together in just the right way, in a specific order. A simple T-shirt may require ten-odd sewing steps, and more-complicated pieces of clothing, such as jeans, involve thirty or more steps. What's more, even for something as seemingly simple as a T-shirt, Reebok and other companies change the cut, design, and specifications every season. It would be nonsensical to design machines to automate the job when the job changes in several unpredictable ways every few months. This is why clothing production is not very automated: the most cost-effective way to make clothing still involves people manually cutting the cloth, arranging the pieces in just the right way and in the right order, and putting them through the machines.

Maybe it's hard for machines, but for humans, it sounds easy. And as Mrs. Shen's story shows, the barriers to entry are low. Anyone with a propensity for micromanagement and a small amount of money to buy sewing machines can set up shop. But it's a precarious business. The margins are razor thin and may vanish altogether with something as innocuous as an unfavorable exchange rate fluctuation. Because Mrs. Shen is paid in foreign currency but pays her workers with Lesothan maloti, any appreciation of the local currency works against her. She must agree to take on work at a certain price in foreign currency and then pay her workers before she receives payment for the finished product. She's been lucky over the past couple of years, during which depreciation of the maloti padded her profits. But she would be unwise to count on this indefinitely, because currency appreciation was one of the main culprits in a devastating industry-wide downturn in Lesotho in 2005. That year alone, 14,000 out of 50,000 garment workers lost their jobs as factory after factory shuttered its doors.[2] If such an event were to repeat itself today, Mrs. Shen would have little room to maneuver—her factory's small size and the lack of pricing power that clothing contractors command mean that she would be unable to raise prices in order to maintain margins.

Indeed, the clothing industry is now dominated by a global supply chain within which Mrs. Shen's factory is but one small link. Designs are made by retailers in the United States, Europe, and other developed countries. These are the brand names we've all heard of—Levi's, Kohl's, Reebok, Walmart. Those retailers go to a few giant sourcing firms (one expert I spoke to called them Big Sourcing), located mainly in Hong Kong and Taiwan, to get an agreement to have their designs made by a specified date and at a specified price. Then Big Sourcing turns to Little Contracting— that is, it parcels out the job to a vast network of much smaller factories across multiple countries in Asia, Africa, and Latin America. The sourcing firms agree on a price with these suppliers and send them the patterns and oftentimes even the cloth. The suppliers may in turn subcontract to smaller factories like Mrs. Shen's. At each step, the margins become thinner. As each factory in the chain completes its assigned task, it packs the finished clothes into shipping containers, and a few months later, their contents appear in stores across the developed world.

It's risky to be the link in the clothing value chain that Mrs. Shen occupies: one messed-up order or a slight exchange rate blip could wipe out her profits. But the upside is that she can get out: if conditions become unfavorable for a few months, she can close up shop and leave. Indeed, in 2008, when it seemed that the US Congress might not renew AGOA, the United States' preferential trade terms with Lesotho and other African countries, many small factories like Mrs. Shen's did shut down overnight.[3] An industry of nearly forty firms lost half its members.

For locals, all this is understandably frustrating. As the economists Lawrence Edwards and Robert Lawrence write, "The firms, almost entirely foreign owned, typically provide assembly, packaging and shipping services and depend on their Asian headquarters to generate orders, design the clothes and send them the fabric they need . . . Almost none of the managers are locals and the buyers of fabric and the marketers of the garments and the key strategic corporate decisions are all made thousands of miles away in Asia."[4] However, there is a plus side: this is about as labor-intensive a business model as one can find in manufacturing. It's no accident that the clothing industry is the largest employer in the country. Moreover, it allows people with very little formal education to make a living in jobs that pay modestly but are unlikely to attract expatriates. In fact, even though the factories are largely foreign owned, they employ very few foreigners: 97 percent of the jobs go to locals.[5] (We will meet some of these Lesothan clothing workers in chapter 5.) But the factories are in constant competition with unseen rivals in faraway countries, and the slightest macroeconomic fluctuation could force them to shut down. Is there another way—another sort of business that is less fickle?

On the other side of town, the Formosa denim mill not only looks and feels a world apart, but operates according to a very different logic. Ricky Chang, a tall, straight-backed former Tai-wanese military officer, greets me exactly at the appointed hour in a bright but spare conference room. Along one wall is a rack hold-ing nearly a hundred samples of denim washes, neatly folded over hangers specifying their item number, description ("indigo stretch mercerized"), and something called a "washing ref" ("1. Unwash / 2. Rinse wash / 3. Bio stone wash / 4. Bio stone bleach"). The plastic table and chairs in the conference room are a uniform industrial gray, as is the floor. The only touch of whimsy is that the black curtains on the windows turn out upon closer examination to be made of dark denim.

The Formosa mill is one of three denim mills owned by Nien Hsing Textile Company Limited, a publicly traded corporation based in Taiwan.[6] The company's market capitalization is nearly US$300 million, making it a behemoth compared with Mrs. Shen's factory.[7] The other two are located in Mexico and Taiwan, and Nien Hsing operates seven more clothing factories around the world as well. Its customers are some of the most recognizable names in US shopping malls: Levi's, the Gap, Old Navy, Chil-dren's Place. "We also used to do Walmart orders as well, but that company is too tough!" Ricky tells me with a laugh.[8]

The Formosa denim mill employs 1,200 workers and cost nearly $100 million to create.[9] It is the size of several football fields, with multiple adjoining buildings all covered by roofs of the same bright blue. At first, Ricky politely but firmly refuses to let me out of the conference room to see the rest of the factory. Underneath his easy smile, his military demeanor makes him suspicious of outsiders. But his giant factories are some of the largest I've seen anywhere, America included, and I keep pestering him to let me take a peek. Finally, a few days later, he tells me to come by again, and he summons a lower-level manager to walk me through their cavernous factory. The man-ager is friendly and explains what's going on, but I suspect he's also meant to make sure I don't take pictures of what I'm not supposed to.

We start outside the factory building, at the loading bays. Semi-trailers stacked high with bales of African cotton come from as far away as Tanzania, 2,500 miles away. Inside, the manager runs his hands through a soft pile of newly unloaded raw cotton; I can see dark specks of seeds and other plant debris in the white pile. Giant machines use rapidly circulating air to fluff the cotton in enormous batches and remove the debris, which collect in little dark piles that look like poppy seeds. Other machines take the newly clean cotton and spin it into a soft, loose rope about an inch in diameter, which is then spun into ever-finer gradations on ever larger spools. The result is a millimeter-thick white thread on spools weighing two tons each. Throughout this process, I see only three workers.

The thread is then loaded onto automatic weaving machines. The weaving room holds hundreds of these machines, which clatter noisily as they spit out denim cloth in rolls two yards wide. There are more workers in this room, but nearly everything is automated, so their jobs mainly consist of feeding spools onto the machines as needed. The rolls of cloth then go into a dyeing room, acrid with the smells of bleach and other chemicals used to make the various rinses of denim: dark, light, splotchy, faded, and so on. Once dyed, each batch of cloth is washed and rolled through a frame set at eye level in front of a watchful worker. By my observation, this is the only labor-intensive part of the production process: workers stare at the cloth rolling past and log any nubs or inconsistencies they see. These logs will be given to the factories that cut the denim so that they know which bits of cloth to avoid; after all, no one wants a pair of jeans with a nub on it. When the logs are complete, machines automatically cut the denim into smaller rolls that two people can carry, and warehouse workers sort the rolls into piles destined for various customers.

Throughout the tour, although it was during working hours and the factory was operating at normal capacity, I saw maybe three dozen workers. Part of the reason I saw so few workers is that Formosa's factory is so big that its 1,200 workers seem few and far between. But another part is that Formosa is a capital-intensive rather than a labor-intensive business. A comparison with Mrs. Shen's factory makes this clear. Although Mrs. Shen declined to tell me how much she has invested in her business, it's simple enough to make a rough estimate. We know that the main assets on her books are her sewing machines. An industrial-style sewing machine is typically worth $1,000, making her factory's main assets worth about $250,000. Most likely, some of her machines were purchased secondhand, so this estimate is probably on the high side. Add in a few additional machines, such as the logo stampers to make the Reebok T-shirts, and a generous total would be $300,000. That means Mrs. Shen's total investment is a paltry 0.3 percent of the $100 million involved in the Formosa denim mill. But Mrs. Shen, with her two hundred or so workers, generates one-sixth as many jobs as the Formosa denim mill does. Her factory provides one job per $1,500 invested, whereas Formosa results in one job per $83,000 invested—a whopping fifty-five-fold difference.

But what Formosa's business model lacks in the number of jobs created, it makes up for in the stability of those jobs. Ricky told me that the mill pays workers 1,100 maloti a week, which at the time was equivalent to about $70. That's a bit lower than what Mrs. Shen said she paid her workers, but according to Ricky, it is higher than the going wage in Vietnamese textile mills. Although Nien Hsing has a factory in Vietnam, it cannot relocate its denim plant from Lesotho to Vietnam, because the logistics of moving giant football fields' worth of specialized machinery across continents would be a nightmare, and the process would take years. So although Lesotho's wages are higher than in Vietnam, the difference would have to be much higher for Nien Hsing to shut down in Lesotho move to a cheaper country. Those 1,200 jobs are not a lot for the size of the capital invested, but on the upside, they are likely to stick around.

. . .

Looking at a pair of steel producers in Nigeria offers a similar contrast. Located in the eastern part of the country, Baoyao Steel is a highly labor-intensive steel smelter. Because its machinery is fairly old-fashioned and its input materials are recycled vehicle parts that must be manually broken down by welders, the company employs nearly 500 workers. When I visited, the dark, cavernous factory space was filled with a mountain of detritus, and dozens of people wearing smudged overalls and hardhats were perched on metal hillocks breaking down the steel parts to feed into the smelter. Management declined to tell me how much was invested in the factory, but its 50,000 tons of annual production capacity is on the low end of steel smelting standards.[10]

On the other side of the country, the Tung family's brand-new cold-rolled-steel plant is incredibly capital-intensive. When I walked through the plant, the gleaming surfaces and automated machinery seemed to come from a different world. The Tung plant cost $1.5 billion and at capacity can produce 700,000 metric tons of steel annually.[11] The plant has created jobs for 5,500 workers, but given its capital outlay, it has an even lower rate of job creation per dollar invested than the Formosa denim mill in Lesotho.

As we conclude our walk through these four factories, one might ask: why is it that we can find any clothing or cloth factories at all in Lesotho, when this entire industry has died out in Nigeria? And conversely, what should we make of the fact that Nigeria has multiple steel plants, while Lesotho has none? What drives which products are made where?

Answering these questions requires examining a major divide between the factories in these two countries: by and large, Lesotho factories export, whereas Nigerian ones serve domestic customers. Nearly all of Lesothan production is exported to more developed markets—about 70 percent to the United States, and nearly all the remainder to South Africa.[12] In Nigeria, although the textile mills started off exporting a large proportion of their output, by the early 1990s, they were serving only the domestic market. From then on, they died out because they could not compete with cheaper imports from Asia. Similarly, the Nigerian steel mills of today— whether they are labor-intensive or capital-intensive businesses— serve almost entirely domestic customers. In some sense, factories in Lesotho have to export to make any sizeable sum of money, since Lesotho is too small a market to justify manufacturing much of anything for the domestic market alone. Lesotho's entire 2015 GDP was $2.3 billion—less than what New York City generates in a single day.[13] By contrast, the Nigerian economy is a behemoth: with a 2015 GDP of $487 billion, it's the largest in Africa and more than 250 times the size of Lesotho's economy.[14] Multiple sectors, including a construction industry hungry for ever-larger quantities of steel, are booming. Unlike cloth or clothing, steel is heavy and hence expensive to ship, so factories have cropped up in Nigeria to serve this rising demand.

But beyond the sheer size of the domestic market, there is the question of infrastructure. One reason that the first Asian clothing investors looked to Lesotho in the 1990s, just when their Hong Kong–Chinese textile counterparts were shutting down in Nigeria, was Lesotho's geographic proximity to excellent South African infrastructure. Jennifer Chen, a Taiwanese clothing entrepreneur who first invested in Lesotho in 1989, says, "Our wave of investors specifically sought out the countries bordering South Africa. Although we couldn't invest directly in South Africa, due to its apartheid policies at the time [against which many destination markets had import bans], we knew that if we were close by, we could take advantage of the stellar transport infrastructure, logistics and shipping services, and road network in South Africa."[15] By contrast, the ports in Nigeria are notorious for being among the most corrupt in the world, and the roads in large sections of the country are in general disrepair. The World Economic Forum ranks Nigeria 127th out of 144 countries on transport infrastructure, and the World Bank ranks it 182nd out of 189 on the cost and ease of trading across borders.[16] To be fair, as we saw in the previous chapter, Nigerian products such as the Lee Group's flip-flops are sold all over West Africa, largely through the efforts of small-scale local distributors. Nevertheless, the condition of its infrastructure makes Nigeria an unlikely choice for foreign investors specifically seeking to serve large-scale export markets such as the United States and Europe.

Government policies, too, can make or break ambitions for export-oriented manufacturing. As we've seen, Nigeria enacted protectionist trade policies at arguably the worst possible moment. When its textile manufacturers started to run into problems, the government raised trade barriers, unwittingly removing the need for domestic firms to become more competitive while heightening the incentives for smugglers. This was ill-timed for another reason as well: global trade policies were creating new openings for African manufacturers. The combination of externally imposed and self-inflicted problems prevented Nigeria from truly benefiting from trade access offered by the EU and the United States— access that Lesotho took ample advantage of. First, the Lomé Convention gave tariff-free access to the EU's markets to its former colonies across Africa and the Caribbean. Second, the Multi Fibre Arrangement (MFA) came to govern global textile production, setting quotas for textiles and garments that developing countries could sell to the developed world. Although the arrangement technically applied to all developing countries, only Asian countries consistently hit their quotas. So Asian clothing factories relocated to locales that had ample quota room, including Lesotho. And when the Lomé Convention expired in 1999, and the MFA expired in 2005, the United States came to the rescue. In 2000, it passed the African Growth and Opportunity Act, granting the least-developed countries in Africa tariff-free access to the US market. Lesotho enjoys those benefits to this day.

In short, a host of factors other than labor costs define where and how factories in Africa operate. An entrepreneur's managerial skill set and access to capital determine the choice of a labor-intensive versus a capital-intensive business model, while market size, infrastructure, and national and global trade policy strongly influence the choice of customers, whether local or global. These factors have significant consequences for African economies in terms of job creation, barriers to entry for local entrepreneurs, and potential risks profile for the host economy. As demonstrated by Mrs. Shen's factory versus the Formosa denim mill in Lesotho and Baoyao Steel versus the Tung family's cold-rolled-steel factory in Nigeria, labor-intensive operations tend to create large numbers of jobs for locals, but those jobs may be flighty compared with the ones at more capital-intensive operations. The Lesotho factories, which serve global customers, are subject to cycles in global demand, whereas the Nigerian firms ride the waves of their local economy.

If Chinese investments in manufacturing in Africa are to spark an industrial revolution, African entrepreneurs must get a piece of the pie as industry develops—much the way Mr. Sun and the Mr. Chens became bosses themselves after working for Taiwanese and Japanese firms. We will explore the possibility of creating a class of African factory owners more deeply in chapter 6; for now, it's worth keeping in mind that a nuanced understanding of manufacturing in Africa has implications for public policies to encourage local participation in the sector. Low-interest government loans are helpful but probably not decisive for getting Lesothan entrepreneurs into the clothing business; what is more important is that they acquire the sort of factory-floor management experience that Mrs. Shen has, along with contacts with global sourcing firms and customers. By contrast, in Nigeria, the booming parts of the manufacturing sector—such as ceramics and steel—require mostly capital-intensive business models. For local entrepreneurs to get a piece of this action, they must have access to cheap financing. There is no one-size-fits-all solution to deepen local participation in manufacturing: African countries will need to enact non-uniform policies that match the needs of whatever sort of manufacturing is viable within their borders.

The multiplicity of these business models and considerations may seem complicated, but that actually gives resilience to the industry as a whole. Because Chinese investments in Africa are varied, with different factory clusters using very different survival strategies, they are subject to different risks. Some, like Mrs. Shen's factory in Lesotho, will be sensitive to exchange rate fluctuations. Others, like the Tungs' steel plant in Nigeria, will be sensitive to input commodity prices. Some are sensitive to shifts in global customer demand or taste; others to changes in the domestic market. Shocks—random or not—will inevitably occur, and some clusters will thrive, while others will die out. Thus manufacturing sector growth in Africa will be uneven across countries. This accords with historical experience: northern England, Detroit and Pittsburgh in the United States, and China's eastern seaboard all became manufacturing centers during their country's turn as the Factory of the World. This is not to say that governments cannot shape the development of their manufacturing sectors. Their policies on infrastructure, finance, and trade matter powerfully, for better and for worse. But those policies will act on differing business models in each country, and each of these public-private interactions will be subject to different risks and opportunities.

For individual countries, this can be perilous—Lesotho lost half the members of its biggest industry during a delay by the US Congress in extending a trade policy—but for Africa as a whole, it's a good thing. Unlike the previous generation of manufacturing, this generation is diverse. As a result, it is much more likely to endure and to find new ways to grow.

CHAPTER 4

Taking a Gamble

On Monday, January 18, 2016, at around 7 p.m., smoke was seen coming out of Barry Gu's clothing factory in Lesotho. A friend of Barry's spotted it, snapped a picture with his cell phone, and sent it to Barry over WeChat, the Chinese equivalent of Facebook.

Barry rushed to the scene and called the fire department, but he knew he shouldn't be overly optimistic. There was only one fire truck in the entire country, and it normally sat at the airport, where just six flights arrived or departed each day. The last flight had left three hours earlier, and most likely no one was at the airport.

At around 9 p.m., Lesotho's minister of trade and investment, Joshua Setipa, came to the scene. He had received a message about the fire while he was at an emergency cabinet meeting convened by Prime Minister Pakalitha Mosisili. The country was in the middle of an international crisis: South Africa, Lesotho's sole neighbor, was threatening to close its borders due to a recent high-profile political assassination. Even so, Minister Setipa had come to commiserate with Barry—a sign of just how critical Chinese investment in Lesotho's manufacturing sector had become. He greeted Barry and told him how sorry he was about the fire. Soon he had to return to the cabinet meeting, but others of Barry's friends and acquaintances came to keep him company.

At 10 p.m., the fire truck finally arrived, but it quickly ran out of water. Unluckily for Barry, his factory had just completed a big order, and the finished goods were sitting inside, waiting to be shipped. Compounding his ill fortune, the factory had also received a delivery of cloth just the day before. Barry and his friends could only watch through the night as it all burned to ashes.

The next day, Barry sat in the dingy trailer-turned-office of another of his businesses and tried to calculate what he had lost. He had insurance, but because the fire had occurred when the factory was unusually full of raw materials and finished products, the insured value wasn't high enough to cover the damages. He called his insurance company to ask how long it would take to process his claim and was told that it depended on the Central Bank of Lesotho, the ultimate backer of the policy. Barry tried to look up the bank's phone number, but its website was down.

Meanwhile, Barry's friends, mostly other Chinese business-people, trickled in. They spoke in hushed tones about the spotty business record of the Chinese owner of the warehouse next door, where the fire had originated. There were already rumors, whispered haltingly and accompanied by meaningful raises of the eyebrow, that the warehouse owner had started the fire himself in a desperate attempt to get out from under mounting business obligations. As Barry's friends gossiped, a steady stream of calls came to his two phones. At one point he perfunctorily thanked a caller for his concern in Mandarin while unleashing a stream of Sesotho into the other phone. A moment later, he barked in English to a visitor, "I don't have time for you today!"

In the afternoon, a reporter from the local radio station came to interview Barry. Amid the still smoking remains of his factory, he stated for the record that he had lost 10 million rand ($590,000), and 330 workers had lost their jobs. He ended by entreating the people of Lesotho to be careful about fire safety. When the radio interview was over, the reporter told Barry that a TV reporter would come to interview him later. Barry's eyes, bloodshot from being up all night, bulged. "Don't make me repeat the same information again," he pleaded. "Don't make me suffer again."

The reporter left, and three of Barry's friends, Chinese men with paunches, closed ranks around Barry and his girlfriend. They launched straight into practicalities. They arranged to have the remaining machinery carcasses stored, in case they could later be salvaged. They discussed where to find housing for the two Chinese workers who had been living on the factory's premises. Barry's girlfriend begged those gathered to help them find jobs in other factories. The friends promised to call the right people. They ordered workers into the burned-out building to remove what remaining equipment they could. Ironically, this included six handheld fire extinguishers.

With all the immediate tasks delegated, Barry turned away and slumped against a pole. One of his friends walked over and pounded him on the shoulder, saying, "I didn't know you were so weak!" Barry raised his head. He sheepishly rejoined the circle. His friend launched into a strange sort of pep talk: "Why are you acting like that? This isn't your only business. And no one was hurt. Besides, which one of us hasn't had a business burn down?" He looked around the circle. "Yup, I have." "Me too." "No question."

Barry gave a weak smile. "I know I'll be okay," he said. "It's just right now, I feel a little down."

. . .

You have to be crazy to run a factory in Africa. Barry's story shows some of the many obstacles, big and small: the lack of a functioning fire brigade, the difficulty of finding a phone number when you need it, the shady neighbors, the geopolitical turmoil, emotional strain that wears down even the hardiest psyche. It's hard work, it's risky, and success is far from assured. In this day and age, the only sizable mass of people crazy enough to take on the job are Chinese people like Barry, fresh from working their way up in factories in China and ready to take a gamble to make their fortune. It takes crazy people like Barry to build a factory in Africa, and that's one of the main reasons Africa's shot at industrialization is tied up with China.

Barry is crazy in one way, but others—such as his neighbor, if the rumors are true—are crazy in a different and much worse way. Some Chinese entrepreneurs bend or break the law, or they find loopholes in Africa's thin regulatory regimes that even if not technically illegal, are nevertheless harmful to African people, environment, or societies. The existence of these Chinese bad actors in Africa is well known, but discussion to date has focused largely on descriptions of—and outrage at—individual or firm-level bad behavior. It's time to understand such behavior in its broader context: the relentless global race in manufacturing. The brutal and thrilling quest to produce ever better goods at ever lower prices, against very real yet seldom seen competitors halfway around the world, sharpens people's edges, producing stark heroism in some and villainy in others. Pressure to become more efficient can easily mutate into pressure to cut corners. Winning this race entails courting risk—with money, with the environment, with human lives.

In this risky, even dangerous, landscape, Chinese entrepreneurs push forward as no one else can. They understand the odds and accept the wild swings of fortune. They survive by building coping mechanisms into the culture: a back-thumping camaraderie that shrugs off fires, a deep-seated resignation that treats misfortune as inevitable even while an irrepressible can-do attitude begins rebuilding before the ashes are cold. Through it all, Chinese entrepreneurs stay the course, and even double down. They are the opposite of Western aid and economic development programs in Africa, all of which basically try to remake Africa into what theory or belief or common sense suggests would be safer or nicer or more conscionable. People like Barry don't indulge in such wishful thinking. They take a gamble on Africa as it is.

. . .

Nowadays, it's hard to survive in the factory business for long. Just ask Alan Lin. He runs the Taiyuan clothing factory in Maseru, Lesotho, across town from Barry's and Mrs. Shen's factories. When I met Alan, he was worried. He assured me this was not out of the ordinary for him: the factory business is a never-ending pile of worries. He was only in his thirties, but he told me that the worries had already made him old. He worries about his customers, his suppliers, his workers. But the most haunting worry of all, the one that has consumed him for a year? Vietnam.

"I went to Vietnam last year to look at clothing factories there," he told me. "I visited one factory that was making Fila brand women's pants, in the exact same style we were." He paused and leaned forward to make sure I understood: "*Exact* same style." A large order had been parceled out to several factories, of which Alan's happened to be one, and the factory he visited in Vietnam another. "Over here in Lesotho, we're using thirty-four steps to make that pair of pants, and we make 600 pairs a day," he continued. "Over there, they use twenty-six steps, and they make a thousand pairs a day."

He chuckled bitterly. "From an efficiency standpoint, from a technical proficiency standpoint, there is a big gap. In the beginning, it was very difficult for us, and we couldn't even make 200 pairs a day of this type of pants. But there's no way out—you have to grit your teeth and keep trying, because the styles keep changing, and it's impossible to survive if you can only make the simple styles. So our workers learned. It was painful, and it took about six months, but they learned, and we went from making 200 pairs a day to 600. But when I went to Vietnam and saw what they were doing there, making a thousand pairs a day, it made me *xia dao le!*"

In Mandarin, *xia dao le* means getting a fright so jolting that it knocks you over.[1]

In 2016, across the clothing industry in Lesotho, this worry about factory-level efficiency was compounded by worries about US trade policy. In February 2016, the United States reached an agreement with Asian countries in negotiations over the Trans-Pacific Partnership, which would lower trade barriers with participating countries. For months before and after, the clothing factory owners in Lesotho could talk about little else. Later in the year, the election of Donald Trump, a strong trade protectionist, effectively killed the deal. But it remains the case that Lesotho's viability as a manufacturing locale depends in part on trade policy set half a world away. As mentioned in the previous chapter, there had been a trade-policy-oriented scare several years earlier, when it looked like the US Congress might not extend Lesotho's tariff-free access to the American market under the African Growth and Opportunity Act. Congress did eventually approve the deal, but not before half of the clothing firms in Lesotho had shut down. For relatively asset-light types of manufacturing such as garment production, any change in conditions can spook at least some manufacturers away to other locales.

I went across town again to talk about global competition with Marina Bizabani, a government official at the Lesotho National Development Corporation. The purpose of her agency is to attract foreign investment to Lesotho and to keep investors happy. Ms. Bizabani was energetic and well-spoken. She declared boldly as soon as we sat down that "we're not worried" about competition from other countries, which made me think that's exactly what she was worried about. In the very next sentence, she let slip, "I always tell my CEO here, 'Let's not worry.'" So at least one high-profile Lesotho government official was, in fact, inclined to worry. And despite her brave front, Ms. Bizabani's agency was acting as if it were worried, spending significant time and resources preparing their case to attract foreign manufacturing investors. It used World Bank funding to engage outside consultants to identify Lesotho's specific areas of comparative advantage. With this information in hand, the agency has aggressively pursued manufacturers in subsectors such as car components and plastics, pitching the fact that Lesotho has lower labor and electricity costs than neighboring South Africa. Clothing factories dominate Lesotho's industrial landscape today; the hope is that attracting other types of manufacturing could help shield the country against another downturn in the clothing industry.[2]

Anxiety about losing foreign firms and intensive efforts to attract more foreign investment are not unique to Lesotho. In Nigeria, I sat down with Amos Y. Sakaba, a director at the Nigerian Investment Promotion Commission, the federal government arm that encourages foreign direct investment into the country—essentially Ms. Bizabani's counterpart. He described how, a few years earlier, his agency had realized that Nigeria could not continue to rely exclusively on its traditional investors from the United States and Europe. It needed to look east, so "as an organization, we started focusing on Chinese and Asian investors." The commission began holding investment forums in almost every province in China, with a particular focus on attracting Chinese manufacturers.

In almost all my conversations with government officials in all four countries discussed in this book, the focus was on attracting and keeping foreign investors. Indeed, the race to become the next Factory of the World is a global one that pits against each other such unlikely match-ups as Nigeria versus Uzbekistan, Lesotho versus Vietnam, and even fellow African countries such as Nigeria versus Ethiopia. These are real examples: before settling on Nigeria as the location for his next factory, Mr. Sun, the ceramics manufacturer from chapter 1, considered Bangladesh, Egypt, Ethiopia, Mexico, and Saudi Arabia as possible locales. He actually owns shares in a ceramics plant in Uzbekistan, so his ongoing capital allocation decisions between Nigeria and Uzbekistan have consequences for workers and governments in both countries. And when I met him, in 2014, he had recently visited Iran and was thinking seriously of building a ceramics plant there as well.[3]

It is no wonder, then, that African government officials are too preoccupied by the ever-present threat of losing these investors to worry about much of anything else. Unless I brought it up, concern that there might be crooks among them who will ruin Africa's environment, corrupt its institutions, and violate its people's rights rarely surfaced.

The image one is left with is of everyone swimming a desperate race amid the choppy seas of global capitalism. Companies and governments are constantly treading water—holding investment promotion fairs in faraway countries, doing studies of their comparative advantages, getting their workers to learn new skills—just to survive. Yet competitors—Vietnam, Uzbekistan—seem somehow to be stronger and faster, and sometimes to kick water in other swimmers' faces, threatening to steal away hard-earned business. And on a grand scale, storms that could engulf everyone—changes in global trade policy or simply an unpredictable shift in American shoppers' tastes—always lurk.

. . .

The fact that manufacturing firms face such stiff competition abroad, coupled with the fact that African government officials spend so much of their finite capacity worrying that they'll lose out on investment from China, creates both the temptation and the opportunity to cut corners. There are many honest Chinese businesspeople in Africa, but others inevitably try to make money in a less than aboveboard way.

Sometimes their practices are not technically even illegal. The thinness of many African regulatory systems means that some practices that would be outlawed in other countries—even

China—are still legal in Africa. A steel mill I visited in Nigeria provides a striking example of a business model that thrives in such an environment. Its machinery was from a decommissioned plant in Shanghai; its owners had bought the plant at a cut rate and shipped it wholesale to Nigeria. The owners could buy the machinery so cheaply because Shanghai had raised its municipal environmental standards for industry, making the plant's technology outdated and unnecessarily polluting. Nigeria didn't yet have environmental laws restricting this sort of factory, so the owners used the same machinery to set up shop there.

This move feels slimy in its failure to respect Nigeria's air and water, but it is not illegal. And the company had struck upon an ingenious model for sourcing raw materials as well. It took the wrecks of old oil tankers off the Nigerian coastline and resmelted them into steel. Given where the company is located, this was a cheap way of sourcing raw materials. It was a win for the Nigerian government as well: the coast guard was highly pleased that someone was dealing with these shipwrecks that had become maritime safety hazards. So although the steel factory was cleaning up Nigeria's coastal waters, it was also polluting Nigeria's air with its unnecessarily dirty operations. This firm is intrinsically neither good nor bad—just intent on making money in whatever way it can.

But some Chinese companies in Africa definitely break the law. On one occasion, it was so brazen that I literally walked right into it.

The Chinatown in Lagos, Nigeria, looks like a child's drawing of a castle. The thick, brick-red walls are evenly crenellated, and the front wall is bracketed by two hulking towers. A pair of flags—the red of the Chinese and the green-and-white of the Nigerian—fly over the front archway. The wall leading to this archway has the slogan "Nigeria–China friendship" painted in large block letters, in both English and Mandarin. But above those letters one can make out the wires of an electrified fence perched on top of the wall, in front of which jagged pieces of glass stand up like teeth.

Inside, it's as if the child has pasted pictures of a strip-mall parking lot and an outdoor market on the drawing of the castle. Cars are parked neatly in the courtyard, under zigzags of bright-red Chinese lanterns. A two-story stack of small shops rings the courtyard, exploding with a colorful array of cheap consumer goods—stall after stall of clothing, makeup, cooking utensils, children's toys.

I was slightly early for my interview with a major Chinese businessman, whom I had never met before. I passed the time by gazing at some bolts of lace. Peach, cream, aqua, powder blue. The listless Nigerian saleslady paid me no mind. Suddenly, a gruff Chinese voice came from an opening between two buildings. "Ah, good, you're here!"

Out popped a middle-aged man, who beckoned me over vigorously.

"Do you speak English?" he asked in Chinese, with no hello or pleasantries.

"Of course," I replied, also in Chinese. "I grew up in the United States."

"Good, good," he said, ushering me into a dark, windowless, smoky room. Two Chinese and a Nigerian sat on assorted sofas, looking at one another. "Could you just translate for them?" asked the businessman whom I'd come to interview. "I'll be back in a bit." Before I could respond, he ducked out of the room.

One of the remaining Chinese looked me up and down, then inquired in Mandarin, "Could you ask him how much it costs to import a forty-foot container of blue jeans into Nigeria?"

I was learning that Chinese folks in Nigeria were not big on greetings. But I played along, relaying the question to the Nigerian in English. After all, I wanted to get my interview.

"Blue jeans are contraband, so it will cost 5.5 million naira [about US$33,000]," the Nigerian explained in English.

I translated for the other two men, who were taken aback by the steep price. They asked me to double-check, but the price remained the same. The Nigerian emphasized again that importing blue jeans was illegal. The men eventually left without committing to a deal, still seemingly shocked at the high sticker price for smuggling.

The businessman I had come to see finally returned and gave me an interview. He didn't mention what I had just witnessed, and I knew better than to ask. To me, the corrupt scene was a reason to sympathize with all the Africans I had spoken to over the years who were angry about the conduct of Chinese businesses in Africa. One prominent Nigerian businessman said to me that same summer, "The Chinese? They taught *us Nigerians* something about corruption! They walk into a government office and throw down bricks of bills, saying 'It's just something to buy a Coke.' "[4] This is from someone used to doing business in a country that ranks 136 out of 168 countries on Transparency International's Corruption Perceptions Index—someone who is difficult to impress when it comes to stories of corruption.[5]

In my interview with the Chinese businessman, I asked him about Nigerian attitudes toward Chinese businesses, but he responded only with generalities about how Chinese businesses can help Nigeria develop, about "Chinese–Nigerian friendship." Eventually, we switched to talking about his own history in Nigeria: setting up multiple businesses and helping many others invest in the country. At first I thought "helping" might be a euphemism for the sort of shady activity I had just witnessed, but as I continued to listen, I realized that there was more to the story. As an early private investor in Nigeria, this man had built a reputation— and a business—by helping other Chinese find footholds in the country. "I provide Chinese businesspeople a platform to get to know Nigeria," he explained. He receives prospective investors at the airport on their first visits to Nigeria, helps them find a place to stay or even hosts them himself, takes them to markets, shopping malls, and other commercial centers to see what's being sold and bought, and gives them a primer on doing business in the country—a personalized Nigeria 101 for the Chinese factory boss. He also acts as a sort of consultant-investor, helping his guests brainstorm and refine business ideas and get their companies up and running. Some of the firms he purports to have nurtured have become enormously successful, including one that pioneered the booming water canister business for home and office use, which was previously nonexistent in Nigeria. That company now employs thousands of people locally.

Put bluntly, the smuggler was also a highly successful venture capitalist.[6] In trendy tech parlance, he could even call himself a startup incubator. He does exactly what he's allowed to do by the circumstances he finds himself in: he smuggles goods because government officials can be bribed, but he also brainstorms inventive business ideas to better serve this fascinating, dynamic market. Without in any way excusing his illegal dealings, we can begin to see why some Chinese businesspeople in Africa resort to corruption. They bet so much in a foreign country—not just in money but in years of their lives spent in unfamiliar and often-times uncomfortable places. They're desperate to recoup their investment and make something to show out of their hardship, so they're tempted when easy ways to cut corners present themselves. We may wish they had more integrity, but they're more amoral than immoral. They do both good and bad things to make their gamble pay off.

. . .

As brazen as Chinese smugglers in Nigeria might be, one could argue that this kind of corruption is in some sense a victimless crime. Not all transgressions are thus. Sometimes there is a very clear victim, a specific person with a name, on whom tragedy falls.

One such name is Kenneth Frederick. In 2013, I was in Nigeria doing research on Chinese business practices there when I heard about the recent death of a Nigerian worker at a Chinese factory. I read the newspapers, which said little beyond the basic outline of what happened. Mr. Frederick had died on the job, electrocuted to death, at a Hong Kong–owned plastic bag manufacturing plant. Beyond that, the question of what had led to his death seemed very much in dispute.

In hopes of better understanding what had happened, I went to see Chinedu Bosah, of the Campaign for Democratic and Workers' Rights, an advocacy group that worked with the employees of that plastic bag factory and helped organize a strike to protest Mr. Frederick's death. His opinion was unequivocal: the company was to blame for Mr. Frederick's death, which was caused by a lack of safety equipment, a paucity of safety training, and an overall hazardous working environment. According to Mr. Bosah, Chinese-owned factories in Nigeria routinely fail to meet safety and other labor standards required by Nigerian law. "You can't ask questions, you can't make phone calls, you stand for twelve hours, you can't talk to each other, you can't even talk to yourself," said Mr. Bosah. "[The workers] are more or less like slaves."[7]

But when I pressed him to say specifically which company actions or inactions had led directly to Mr. Frederick's death, Mr. Bosah admitted that he did not know. He had never been inside the factory, and he had never managed to speak to any of the company managers, either about this incident or about safety concerns in general. That was unsurprising: I had often heard from Chinese managers that they are uncomfortable interacting with the press and unions—two types of organizations that don't exist in unfettered form in China. They are especially skittish about giving interviews or having meetings in English, a language in which they feel they can easily be misunderstood.

By asking around in the Chinese community in Lagos, I managed to connect with a senior manager, whom I will call Mr. S., overseeing the plastic bag plant where Mr. Frederick died. Without bringing up Mr. Frederick, I said I was interested in visiting the plant (which was true—I visited a dozen Chinese firms on that trip), and he agreed to show me around. Inside the plant, more than 500 workers were busy feeding the machines that made plastic bags, packing the finished bags in bundles for customers, and doing various other jobs on the factory floor. The workers wore uniforms, but they didn't wear gloves while handling the hot plastic bags. And despite a sign on the wall about the importance of safety boots, most of them wore flip-flops.

During a lull in the conversation during lunch, I cautiously brought up the issue of worker safety. I asked about the factory's safety standards, including the discrepancy between the sign about boots and the flimsy footwear I had just observed. Mr. S. said that the company issued two pairs of boots every year to each worker, but many workers refused to wear them or even took them outside the factory and sold them.

I pressed on, bringing up Mr. Frederick's death. Mr. S. sighed heavily and explained that it had been caused by Mr. Frederick's own disregard for the company's safety instructions. He said that the company had nevertheless paid for Mr. Frederick's funeral and other expenses. Mr. S. expressed regret that the Chinese manager in charge of the factory had not communicated publicly about what had happened, shutting himself within the factory walls because of his discomfort with expressing himself in English to the press.

As far as I know, I am the only person to have spoken to both sides of the dispute over Mr. Frederick's death. In fact, when I told Mr. Bosah about my visit to the plastic bag factory, he was surprised that Mr. S. had spoken to me at all; Mr. Bosah himself had long since given up trying to get through to management. The press, too, had only covered one side of the story, because the Chinese factory manager refused to make public statements. And to the best of Mr. Bosah's and Mr. S.'s knowledge, local government officials had also not investigated the matter deeply.[8]

This is the structural tragedy that brings about individual tragedies like Mr. Frederick's. Industrialization requires factories like this plastic bag plant, whose primary concern is to make money. The countries that most need these factories for economic development tend to have the fewest resources for investigating and preventing such tragedies, and those resources are more often allocated to attracting additional investors than to carefully regulating the ones that are already there. As a result, we may never know why Mr. Frederick died. We can only be sure that there will be more Mr. Fredericks as Africa industrializes.

. . .

Taken all together—the pressure and worry about global competition on one side, thin regulations and enforcement capacity on the other—the result is a combustible state of affairs that poses acute dangers to the health and well-being of Africans. Global competition tempts countries to give foreign investors ever more incentives to invest—tax holidays for attracting firms to special economic zones are a favorite these days—and possibly to not look too closely when labor or environmental incidents occur. This raises the specter of a sort of race to the bottom—that with the arrival of each new factory, labor and environmental standards will lower, and the benefits to receiving countries will decrease. And attracting and keeping foreign investors takes government officials an enormous amount of time, stealing scarce human capital from other important tasks, such as investigating troubling incidents or even designing smart regulations to prevent such incidents in the future. In the absence of appropriate regulations and the capacity to monitor what's going on, countries are likely to end up with at least a few ethically or environmentally unscrupulous investors. As we have seen, manufacturing entrepreneurs undertake risky and sometimes dangerous enterprises, and the pervasive pressure under which they live causes some of them to resort to questionable tactics in order to beat the odds.

In this intense and resource-scarce context, how can rampant corruption, excessive pollution, and deaths like Mr. Frederick's be prevented? The Western development community's conventional answer has been to invest in governance programs in developing countries: training for government officials, monitoring and accountability systems, even external consultants paid to work as part of developing-country bureaucracies. The goal is essentially to make those bureaucracies function as their counterparts in developed countries do. These programs are well-intentioned, and no doubt some of them have saved other workers from Mr. Frederick's fate. Yet overall, they're ineffective. In a "synthesis report" assessing the track record of transparency and accountability programs in developing countries, the authors write, "Despite their rapid growth, and the growing donor support they receive, little attention has been paid to the impact and effectiveness of these new transparency and accountability initiatives."[9] That was written very tactfully, no doubt because the study was funded by some of the top Western donors, including the Department for International Development (the UK's international aid agency), the Ford Foundation, and the Omidyar Network. A less tactful way to put it would be to say that the donors have been funding these programs without regard to whether they actually work. So do they? After reviewing the results of the top 75 studies in the field, all the report's authors could muster in support of these programs is that there is "some emerging evidence of impact, though limited and uneven."[10] The tactless translation: sort of, but not really.

The lessons of the past suggest another, albeit more painful, way forward. Rather than curbing industrialization to prevent its excesses, the experience of countries that have already developed show that paradoxically, further industrialization that leads to further excesses is what eventually creates the political and social pressures for regulation and reform. The history of labor protection laws in the United States makes this abundantly clear. Basic safety regulations were enacted only *after* horrific industrial accidents galvanized the public to press for reform. In 1911, a fire erupted at the Triangle shirtwaist factory, where young female workers had been locked in by an unsympathetic foreman, killing 146 young women in the deadliest workplace accident in New York City's history. This tragedy was also the city's deadliest building fire until September 11, 2001. Only in its sad aftermath were thirty-six new state laws regulating workplace safety conditions passed, even though the young women who worked and died in the factory had been agitating for better conditions for a year before the fire.[11] Similarly, it took six disastrous mine blasts in 1940 for the US government to finally begin mine inspections.[12] The point is not that these accidents were somehow necessary, or that we shouldn't work toward better working conditions and accident-prevention mechanisms, but that history shows effective regulation to always come *after* industrialization swings into full motion, not before.

This is a difficult thought. Even assuming that African nations will protect their workers better than previously industrializing countries did, industrialization practically guarantees that people will die, some in truly horrific ways. We are tempted to think that Africa should back away from the path of industrialization. Every human life is precious, with value that is incommensurate with the dollars and cents of business success and GDP growth. But that would be—dare I say it—a romanticized view from countries in which the clanging steel and ugly machine parts and the blood and guts of early-stage industrialization have already faded into a bygone era. For those who lived it, who experienced it, who have paid the ultimate price, the need to forge ahead, to build more factories in the ashes of destroyed ones, is obvious. This is why Africa's best chances for development lie neither with Western development programs nor with airbrushed Chinese government efforts. Instead, its future is bound up with gruff, unpretty Chinese factory bosses. Because when these people get knocked down, they get up again and fight on.

. . .

The day after the fire, after Barry's friends had thumped him on the back and told him in no uncertain terms to buck up, I tagged along with one of them as the group dispersed. Mr. Wu is a bald, middle-aged man with round, shiny cheeks. He was wearing shorts and a blue T-shirt with a pattern of tiny navy flowers and a large Uzzi logo across his chest, above the slogan "Durability & Strength." As we talked, his brassy voice erupted in energetic crescendos, accompanied by animated hand gestures. Both his pinky fingers and one ring finger had nails an inch long—the sign of a boss whose work allows for carefully manicured long nails rather than the short nails of a manual laborer.

It turned out that Mr. Wu could look Barry in the eye and tell him to take heart because he himself was no stranger to misfortune, and to rebuilding after events that would sideline others for years or even a lifetime. He had arrived in Lesotho in June 1998 and poured $46,000 of his savings into a store that sold shoes, aluminum pots, and other light consumer goods. In September of that year, his store burned to the ground. He revived his business and eventually expanded it into a successful supermarket, but a few years later, disaster struck again. His supermarket was robbed, and in the fracas his father was shot dead. A few years after that, his brother, whom he had encouraged to move from China to help him with the business, was killed in a gas explosion. Through it all, Mr. Wu forged ahead; he continued to operate his supermarket and now also owns two factories.

Perhaps it is no accident that the original meaning of the word *undertaker* referred to businesspeople. In the fifteenth century, the word *undertaker* meant contractor, or anyone who undertook a task. Only later did the word become primarily associated with funeral directors. In modern German, *unternehmer* ("undertaker") still means "entrepreneur." It's a reminder that entrepreneurship still fundamentally involves undertaking difficult tasks, which involves undertaking risk, which sometimes involves undertaking death.

In Lesotho, with the ashes of his friend's factory not yet cold, Mr. Wu leaned forward. "My blood—my family's blood—is in this country," he said. He regarded me with a look of determination. "Where you get knocked down is where you have to get back up."[13]

PART TWO

POSSIBILITIES

CHAPTER 5

On the Line

Ahmed Ibrahim, a tall, dark-skinned man, moved gracefully through the cardboard box factory. As he showed me around, it was immediately clear that he knew everything about making cardboard. He knew the pulp suppliers, he knew how to unload the materials, he knew every piece of machinery, he knew the latest customer orders, he knew how to fix a print run that had an offset, and he knew all the workers. His boss, the owner of the factory, is Chinese, but everyone knows that it's Ahmed who really runs things.

Ahmed started at the bottom. He is from Sokoto, one of the poorest states in Nigeria. After secondary school, like many Nigerian young men, he was underemployed and surviving by working odd jobs. Because he had grown up near the border with Niger, he spoke French, and he found a niche buying cars from the French-speaking Lebanese car dealers in Benin on behalf of Nigerians who wanted to take advantage of Benin's much lower import duties. It was unsteady work, but it was something. In 2009, Ahmed got a call from a Chinese man he had once met on the street. This man had a buddy, Mr. Wang, who was fresh from China and hoped to start a business in Nigeria. Ahmed agreed to work for Mr. Wang, first as a driver, then quickly morphing into a sort of all-purpose local fixer.

The key moment in Ahmed's career came when Mr. Wang wanted to buy a car for his fledgling company the way local Nigerians did, bypassing Nigeria's high import tariffs via Benin. Ahmed would have to do it—Mr. Wang certainly did not know French, which was needed to negotiate with the Lebanese car dealers. But could Ahmed be trusted with so much money? Mr. Wang's Chinese managers fretted. Finally, in a split-second decision, Mr. Wang locked eyes with Ahmed and handed over the full amount for a brand-new vehicle, in cash. As Ahmed left for Benin, all Mr. Wang's Chinese employees shook their heads in disbelief, convinced they had seen the last of Ahmed and the cash.

To their surprise, Ahmed came back a couple of weeks later with the car—and change. He was full of apologies, however, because he had spotted—in his own words—a pair of "beautiful shoes that could not be resisted," so he had used some of the change to buy them. While the Chinese employees were still in complete shock that Ahmed had come back at all, Ahmed went on and on about how bad he felt that he had used his boss's money for a pair of shoes without permission. He insisted that this amount be docked from his next paycheck. Needless to say, Mr. Wang was not upset in the least about the shoes, and from that day on, Ahmed was his right-hand man.[1]

As time passed, with his loyalty and work ethic beyond question, Ahmed was entrusted with increasing amounts of responsibility at the factory. Soon he was running its day-to-day operations. Mr. Wang favored him so much that, unprompted, he came in one day with business cards identifying Ahmed as "Manager." The Chinese person with the same title was insulted. Ahmed, wanting to keep the peace and recognizing that he had de facto authority anyway, quietly stopped using the business cards.

There is no question that working in the cardboard box factory has transformed Ahmed's life. In his tribe, men need a certain amount of wealth to get married, and before working at the factory, Ahmed had no choice but to remain single. Now he has not one but two wives (polygamy is accepted in his tribe), cementing his status as a rich man. And in his capacity as de facto plant manager, he brought his younger brother Ishmael into the business. Ishmael has learned the ropes quickly and can already run the plant on his own on days when Ahmed is taking care of other business for Mr. Wang. As we walked through the plant together, Ahmed spoke to the workers in Hausa, a language from northern Nigeria not normally spoken in the central part of the country where the factory is located. It turns out that they were speaking Hausa because the workers weren't from the surrounding area. Ahmed had literally brought his village to work.

This is perhaps the most tantalizing possibility that becoming the next Factory of the World holds for Africa: full employment for its hitherto chronically underemployed but burgeoning population. The hope is that factories can provide jobs not just for rare remarkable individuals like Ahmed, but as in this case, for entire villages. Yet, as we shall see, this possibility feels deeply uncertain, even to some of those closest to the transformation. Throughout Africa, Chinese bosses complain about their African workers; even those who grew up working in factories themselves tend to forget how hard it is to get used to factory work. And it is easy for people in industrial and post-industrial societies, ourselves included, to forget how many profound transitions are unleashed when someone goes to work in a factory. History shows that industrialization has fundamentally transformed every society it has touched. Africa, now feeling the first reverberations of its coming, will be no exception. For the continent, mass employment will involve not simply economics, but also social and political changes that will remake the very underpinnings of society.

. . .

But first, let's examine the extent of the employment involved. The common perception in Africa and the sentiment in African media is that Chinese firms don't hire Africans. Many suspect racist motivations; there is even an unfounded but remarkably persistent rumor that some Chinese firms bring prisoners from China rather than making local hires.[2] The McKinsey research study I recently co-led collected the largest data set ever to address this question, which showed that Chinese companies in Africa overwhelmingly hire locals. Across a sample size of more than 1,000 Chinese firms employing more than 300,000 people, 89 percent of employees were Africans.[3] In manufacturing, this proportion is even higher, at 95 percent. Moreover, previous studies show that the longer Chinese companies operate in Africa, the higher their proportion of local hires.[4] This suggests that what Ahmed experienced may be a more general phenomenon: as Chinese bosses get to know locals over time, they entrust them with more responsibilities.

For Africa, many more factories—and hence jobs—will most likely come out of Chinese investment over the next decade. Demographic factors, rising energy costs, and increasing competition are already eroding profits for factory owners in China and pushing them to relocate. A generation under the one-child policy has shrunk China's labor pool, causing shortages in its coastal manufacturing hubs. Labor costs in China have risen sharply in recent years: since 2001, manufacturing hourly wages have increased by 12 percent each year.[5] At the Eighteenth Party Congress, in October 2012, the Chinese government set a target of doubling per capita income by 2020, all but ensuring that those wages will continue to rise in the future.[6] And although the productivity of Chinese manufacturing workers has grown substantially, productivity-adjusted wages grew nearly threefold from 2004 to 2014. Energy prices have also risen: the cost of electricity grew by 66 percent and the cost of natural gas more than doubled during this period.[7] The writing is on the wall: many more Chinese facto-ries will soon have no choice but to relocate to other countries. As Mr. Wu, the general manager of Skyrun, a Chinese home appli-ances brand with assembly operations in Nigeria, told me, "Sooner or later, we will have to relocate our factories away from China. The trend of global manufacturing sites is to shift. First it was the West, then East Asia, and now it's shifting to other countries."[8]

To be clear, an enormous number of jobs are at stake. If Africa becomes China's successor as the next Factory of the World, it could completely eliminate unemployment. According to Justin Yifu Lin, the former chief economist of the World Bank, "Having itself been a 'follower goose,' China is on the verge of graduat-ing from low-skilled manufacturing jobs and becoming a 'lead-ing dragon.' That will free up nearly 100 million labor-intensive manufacturing jobs, enough to more than double manufacturing employment in low-income countries."[9] To put that further into perspective, when the United States reached its peak in manu-facturing employment, in 1978, only 20 million Americans were working in factories.[10] Now five times that number are about to come out of a single country: China.

This flood of jobs coming out of China matches Africa's current demographic moment. Ahmed and his brother Ishmael were rep-resentative of Africa's population in general: young and underem-ployed. Already, 30 percent of the sub-Saharan African population is in the ten-to-twenty-four age bracket, and the demographic momentum from so many people at or nearing reproductive age will carry forward several generations, even if birthrates come down.[11] But because it has such high birthrates—in fact, the high-est in the world—Africa is on the brink of an unprecedented pop-ulation explosion. According to United Nations projections, the sub-Saharan African population will double from roughly 1 bil-lion in 2015 to more than two billion by 2050.[12] Nigeria alone, which had a population of only 45 million at independence, in

1960, will have nearly 400 million people by 2050, surpassing the US population.[13]

Before he met Mr. Wang, Ahmed had trouble finding a steady job. Sadly, his experience is common in Africa today. African nations already have some of the highest unemployment rates in the world.[14] In Nigeria, the official rate is 12.1 percent, but the government recognizes an additional 19.1 percent of the working-age population as underemployed.[15] For young people, the situation is much worse: a distressingly high 42.2 percent.[16] In addition, continent-wide, 77.4 percent of those lucky enough to be employed have what the International Labour Organization calls "vulnerable jobs"—those without formal working arrangements and likely to lack decent working conditions and job security.[17] According to the World Bank, 90 percent of the jobs created in Africa today are in the informal sector—the very ones that lead to vulnerability rather than a stable path to the middle class.[18] Add in the demographic bulge that will double Africa's working-age population, and it's easy to see that the continent is facing an acute need for formal job creation of the sort that factories bring.

Why specifically those jobs? Because manufacturing jobs are unlike other jobs, and they're more important for Africa than other types of jobs are. Manufacturing forms a significant proportion of what's called the traded sector (as opposed to the non-traded sector, which includes most local services, such as restaurants, shops, construction, and even highly paid professionals like doctors and lawyers). The distinction is important: the traded sector tends to be more productive and to become ever more so over time because its output must compete globally, whereas local services don't. Economists know that in the long run, the only way to achieve higher standards of living is through higher productivity. What's more, manufacturing drives demand for other jobs: for every manufacturing job that's created, 1.6 service jobs follow.[19] As Ron Bloom, senior counselor for manufacturing policy under President Obama, put it, "If you get an auto assembly plant, Walmart follows; if you get a Walmart, an auto assembly plant does not follow."[20] For Africa, job creation in the agricultural or services sector is okay, but job creation in the manufacturing sector is what's really needed.

Furthermore, beyond their sheer numbers, the types of jobs involved in manufacturing are enticing. Neither Ahmed nor his brother Ishmael went to college or to any vocational or technical training school. What formal education they did have, in elementary and secondary school, was in a chronically underfunded system in one of the poorest states in a poor country. Yet things might have been even worse for them: according to the Brookings Institution, most of the world's children who are not enrolled in primary school are Africans. Furthermore, when African children are in school, they are not learning: more than a third of them are not acquiring basic skills in literacy and numeracy.[21] Unsurprisingly, the educational outcomes at these schools are truly appalling—Africa has the highest rate of illiteracy of any region in the world.[22] According to the African Development Bank, half the students who graduate from these schools are unskilled, and that is unlikely to change given the strain on these school systems from both a budgetary and a human resources standpoint.[23]

Given all this, one way to understand the potential impact of Africa's becoming the next Factory of the World is to recognize that good factory jobs are one of the few ways that Africa can realistically make up for its bad schools. As a former public school teacher in Africa, it pains me to write this. But the unfortunate state of the school that Ahmed attended—and of the colleges he never had a chance to go to—means that he never had a shot at becoming an accountant, or a doctor, or a software engineer. Driving cars from Benin to Nigeria was a marginal existence— one that did not allow him to start a family, or take care of the one he already had. Doing well in Mr. Wang's factory opened all these possibilities for Ahmed: a steady income, an address to call home, status in his community, security for his family.

. . .

To be clear, Ahmed is a remarkable person, and his story is a remarkable case. How many more Chinese bosses will give other Africans a shot, as Mr. Wang did for Ahmed? Even Mr. Wang, who enabled, benefited from, and witnessed firsthand Ahmed's transformation from odd-jobs handyman to factory manager, isn't at all sure that training more Nigerians will yield similarly good results. "Sure, there's a lot of smart Nigerians," he told me. "But overall, the education level is very . . . low."[24] I understood this to be Mr. Wang's polite, hesitant way of saying he viewed Ahmed as an exception, not the rule.

Down the road, some other Chinese factory owners were more blunt. "The locals are lazy," one declared baldly. "We fire a lot of people, especially in their first month on the job. They don't even show up on time, or they don't come every day, yet they expect to be paid!"[25] His Lebanese neighbor, the owner of a steel mill, concurred. "Two Chinese workers are worth five Nigerians," he insisted.[26] Across the continent, in East Africa, an Indian-Kenyan factory owner offered a hierarchy of ratios: "I need two Kenyan workers to do the work of one Indian worker, but it would take me four Tanzanians to do the same work," he said.[27]

In interviews with factory owners across Africa, I heard similar complaints all the time—so often, in fact, that I eventually stopped noting them. Why are factory owners, even the ones who have had good experiences with local workers, so down on them? Do these attitudes jeopardize Africa's chances of becoming the next Factory of the World? And even if Africa does manage to attract more factories, will such frictions prevent them from creating mass employment for Africa's booming population?

The easy answer as to why factory owners—Chinese in particular—have such a low opinion of African workers is that they are racist. This has been well noted by journalists reporting on the Chinese in Africa: Howard French has described a "kind of casual primary racism by Chinese newcomers toward Africans."[28] Indeed, some of the comments I've picked up remind me of nothing so much as puerile playground insults that are all the more intractable because of their senselessness. An example: "Nigerians complain that Chinese people spit. But they pee in public on the side of the road all the time!"[29]

Nevertheless, there are also signs that people are adjusting, mixing, getting used to one another, even as they cling to arbitrary race-based distinctions. One evening, at dinner in a hole-in-the-wall Chinese restaurant in Addis Ababa, our Ethiopian waitress stonewalled us when I asked for fried rice.[30] Refusing to believe that a Chinese restaurant anywhere in the world didn't have fried rice, I asked to speak to the Chinese owner. Because I was with international friends, I had been speaking English, so the waitress was surprised when I said I was Chinese. "You're Chinese!" she exclaimed with a wide smile, as if I had revealed that I was her long-lost sister. The owner came along and apologized profusely, assuring us that since I was Chinese, we could have fried rice. "I don't serve my fried rice to locals," he explained, as if that should be obvious. Just then, a wide-eyed, curly-haired toddler waddled up to the Chinese man and the Ethiopian woman and patted both of them on the legs. It turned out that he was their son. On one level, the situation was absurd: fried rice for locals is out of the question, whereas starting a family with one is not. But on another level, it demonstrated the kinds of changes occurring as Chinese and Africans interact in new situations. That couple is living a life unimaginable not only to their parents but also, most likely, to their younger selves. Strikingly progressive attitudes are forming even as old habits die hard. In view of all the bracingly new thoughts and feelings the couple in the restaurant must navigate in their pioneering way of life, the fact that they've thus far neglected to update their fried rice policy seems more understandable.

Indeed, what's often mistaken for simple racism is more complicated. The ugly comments by Chinese factory owners about African workers have a universal quality that may reflect the timeless tensions of industrialization more than disdain between races. In 1821, for example, at the height of the Industrial Revolution, a British writer described English manual workers with alarm: "We shall often see them just simply annihilating those portions of time . . . [they] yielded up to utter vacancy and torpor . . . practicing some impertinence, or uttering some jeering scurrility, at the expense of persons going by."[31] *Vacancy, torpor, scurrility*: that's certainly a more impressive vocabulary, but the fundamental sentiment is the same as what we hear in Africa today, without race figuring into the equation at all, since everyone involved was Caucasian. Indeed, other well-educated British commentators fretted about the laziness of workers, who whiled away entire days with little urgency: "[T]he hand-loom went to the slow chant of *Plen-ty of Time, Plen-ty of Time*" and few resisted the "temptation to lie in an extra hour in the morning."[32] Apparently, English workers not only were lazy on the job but also missed entire days of work; Mondays in particular were popular for not showing up. The great labor historian E. P. Thompson noted, "There are few trades which are not described as honouring Saint Monday: shoemakers, tailors, colliers, printing workers, potters, weavers, hosiery workers, cutlers, all Cockneys. Despite the full employment of many London trades during the Napoleonic Wars, a witness complained that 'we see Saint Monday so religiously kept in this great city . . . in general followed by a Saint Tuesday also.'"[33]

But this antagonistic adolescent phase of British industrialization soon passed, as English workers became the first to figure out how to mold themselves to machine rhythms en masse. As soon as they did so, they became the envy of industrialists elsewhere in Europe. In our day and age, the German factory worker epitomizes industrial precision and discipline, but scholars are unequivocal that there was a time in which "the difficulties were great" in using German laborers for factory work. Factory owners in Germany were described as casting "admiring and envious glances . . . across the Channel at the English industrial worker."[34] Fast forward a century, and the same complaints abound in the early days of Chinese industrialization. In 1991, around the time that I first sat in a car, the *Wall Street Journal* reported that the "Chinese lack work ethic . . . Most Chinese employees spend as much as half their eight-hour workdays goofing off."[35]

The point is that factory owners have always complained about their workers during the early phases of industrialization, and Chinese bosses in Africa today are no exception. That's because they're accustomed to managing workers from their own country. They experience the fact that workers from the new country are less productive, and they reach for race as the explanation, when in fact the new workers simply haven't been industrialized as long as workers in their home country have. As Alexander Gerschenkron, the great Ukrainian-born scholar of European industrialization, put it: Although "the cheapness of labor in a backward country is said to aid greatly in the process of industrialization . . . the overriding fact to consider is that industrial labor, in the sense of a stable, reliable, and disciplined group that has cut the umbilical cord connecting it with the land and has become suitable for utilization in factories, is not abundant but extremely scarce in a backward country. Creation of an industrial labor force that really deserves its name is a most difficult and protracted process."[36] The lesson of history is that industrial labor, as distinct from merely cheap labor, is often in *short* supply in unindustrialized economies, and factory owners in the first throes of industrialization have always complained bitterly about this fact.

There is no doubt that some Chinese factory owners in Africa are racist. But these eerily similar historical comparisons reveal that their disparaging comments about African workers reflect something more. In many societies, factories are the sites where different classes and cultures rub together for the first time, and they must do so in the process of performing truly difficult work, in the context of brutal global competition. Factories are also where workers are confronted with unrelenting new norms and evaluated for the first time according to machine rather than human standards. The bitterness behind these comments is a refraction of the hard essence of industrialization, a human struggle at the heart of this profound transformation.

What is the nature of this human struggle? One characteristic is so obvious that we tend to forget it: working on a manufacturing line is, well, a struggle. It's genuinely hard. In an age when Americans rue the decline of Detroit and politicians rail against trade deals that might ship manufacturing jobs abroad, it is easy to romanticize factory work. And although factory work of the classic sort—performing the same motions again and again on an assembly line—does not require high educational attainment, it does not follow that it's *easy*. It is a fraught process to mold the human body, with its nonuniform impulses, and the human mind, with its random wanderings, to a rigid machine rhythm. Factory jobs require manual dexterity, an overriding sense of discipline, and incredible endurance. "Nothing is as hard as being an ordinary worker" was a mantra often repeated by one of the workers that the journalist Leslie Chang profiled in her portrait of factory life in China.[37] Most Americans today have forgotten this, but their parents and grandparents knew it. Views of the factory from another age, when many more Americans were actually working in factories, reveal a different reality. In the 1936 film *Modern Times*, Charlie Chaplin plays a factory worker trying to survive on the line. He stops for a split second to scratch his armpit, and he's immediately behind. He's yelled at by the line supervisor, and when he talks back, it puts him even further behind. He catches up, only to have a fly buzz irksomely before his eyes, disturbing his vision and putting him behind yet again. He catches up once more, but his wrench becomes stuck on a passing product, forcing the whole line to shut down. As he walks away to take a break, his muscles continue to twitch in the same machine rhythm. It's funny, because Chaplin was a comedic genius; but like all comedies, it has a kernel of truth at its heart. The line is relentless, and factory work is hard.

. . .

There is another reason that workers everywhere who encounter industrialization find it to be such a struggle. Industrialization alters traditional societies in irrevocable ways. It is no accident that we call these transformations industrial *revolutions*. What happens on the line changes every aspect of life off the line.

One classic example is a radically different notion of time. Pre-industrial societies pace themselves by the sun and the seasons. People are task oriented: no great stock is put in precise timing, as long as the necessary work gets done. But factories run on clock time, and precision is of the essence. Being clock oriented means that one minute late is late nonetheless, and can get you fired. E. P. Thompson documented that wherever factories showed up in eighteenth-century Britain, fights broke out between workers and employers as workers protested enslavement by the clock. The conflict was accompanied by an incessant stream of badmouthing on both sides: even as workers felt trapped by the alien rigidity of clock time, their bosses fumed that they couldn't seem to do something as simple as show up on time. Thompson wrote, "The stress of the transition falls upon the whole culture: resistance to change and assent to change arise from the whole culture. And this culture includes the systems of power, property-relations, religious institutions, etc."[38] In this light, Chinese manufacturers' complaints about their workers sound like an echo of the original howl of industrialization itself. An entire society is being dragged from a way of life that moves with the sun to one that ticks according to clocks and calendar invites.

It was hard for British workers in the eighteenth century to undergo such fundamental shifts in their way of life, and it is hard for African workers today. Conforming to the demands of the factory requires a fundamentally different way of organizing the rest of one's life. And with global competition bearing down, the transformation taking place in Africa today is, if anything, faster-paced and more relentless.

Mpho Agatha Kanono is a thirty-five-year-old woman with shiny cheeks and a wide, easy smile. She is from a rural village in Lesotho, and at age twenty-one, shortly after having a baby, she went to work in a clothing factory. After two years, she was fired unfairly, so she moved across the country to work in another factory. Altogether, she spent ten years working in clothing factories, mainly for Chinese bosses.

In an age-old refrain about how factory work takes a worker's time and makes it the company's time, she told me about once having to stay in the factory and work for more than twenty-four hours straight. "One day, I heard the beating." Mpho smacked her fist against her palm: *thwack, thwack, thwack.* She continued her story in a dignified cadence: "The director of the factory, who was Chinese, was beating my supervisor, who was also Chinese. And because of that, we had to work overtime. We began at 7 a.m., and we spent the night there and came out at lunchtime, at 12 p.m. the next day."

I asked if she had been paid overtime for that work, and she said yes. Knowing that she had a young child at home, I then asked if she'd had advance notice that she would be required to work all night. She just laughed. "Because the Chinese was under pressure, he came and begged us: 'Please stay. You see that I'm in trouble,'" she explained. "If your boss begs you, you're supposed to help him."

Mpho's story reveals several profound and concurrent transformations, all unleashed by factory work. There's the loss of agency over her time—a new demand that she reorganize her life around the needs of the factory, even at a moment's notice. There's the necessity to redefine motherhood—Mpho has to find overnight child care when she works nights at the factory, and she has to bring up her daughter in an environment with a rhythm and constraints very different from those she herself was brought up with. There's the remarkable degree of empathy she has developed: a young woman from a rural village, she nevertheless learned quickly to understand the pressures bearing down on a Chinese factory supervisor. And there's the need to move: after losing her first job, she had to relocate to find another one—reflecting the larger phenomenon of migration from the countryside to the city.

But where there is a loss of control, there may also be the seeds of a new agency. A few days before I met Mpho, I had gone to visit the Independent Democratic Union of Lesotho (IDUL), the largest garment workers' union in the country. Toward the end of an interview about the union's activities and workers' conditions in general, I brought up the issue of gender within the union with Mr. Solong Senohe, IDUL's general secretary, and Mr. Daniel Maraisane, its international coordinator. I had walked through enough Lesothan clothing factories to know that three-quarters of garment workers are women, so I was curious about the fact that all the IDUL staff members I'd met in their offices were men. First I asked in innocuous terms how Mr. Senohe and Mr. Maraisane had come to join the clothing union; I was surprised to learn that neither of them had ever worked in a clothing factory. Like many other men involved in Lesotho's clothing unions, they had become active in the movement by working in South African mines, famous for breeding powerful unions that are active and often decisive in South African politics.

It made a certain amount of sense that Lesotho's nascent movement was an offshoot of South Africa's strong union tradition. But I was still curious to hear whether any women were among IDUL's leadership. In response to my questions, the two told me to come back the next day.

When I returned, Mpho was waiting to meet me. Unlike the men's, her story of becoming involved in the union was much more direct: the union that was supposedly representing her had done nothing when she was unfairly fired from her first factory job, so she'd been determined to take matters into her own hands. In her next job, she started helping to organize her coworkers to try to make sure what happened to her would not happen again. She had become a shop steward, the union representative on the factory floor—that linchpin figure responsible for signing up workers, collecting dues, and channeling grievances. She had spent nearly eight years working in a clothing factory while also being active in the union, so when the factory she worked in closed, the union asked her to join as a full-time organizer.

I met two other female union organizers that day: Mampoi and Mopa. Mampoi had become active in the movement after experiencing discrimination at the factory where she worked. Mopa had worked at a denim factory for years before being fired, but still organized workers there to demand improved conditions. Her highest-priority demand? Heaters in the winter. She worked hard on strikingly practical issues: getting certain doors opened for more ventilation, instituting health and safety training, providing hot water during the winter. Whereas the men in the union had emphasized wage and overtime issues, Mopa cared about the day-to-day concerns of workers whose waking hours were spent mostly in factories.

Toward the end of the conversation, I brought up the fact that the top union leaders were all men. The three women nearly leaped out of their chairs in excitement. While working in factories and organizing for the union, they had observed some of the structural issues affecting the labor movement in Lesotho. What's more, they aspired to fix them. "If you understand the history of textile trade unionism in Lesotho, they are all split because the leaders are the men," said Mopa, referring to the competition and infighting between various clothing unions. She continued, "Maybe we can come with the solution: talk like females, and see things as females. Now we try to convince them that we, as the women officials, we want to be part of the decisions of the union." At another point in the conversation, she appealed to me directly: "How can you help us, Irene? To motivate us and help us to get more power, more power, more power!"

I was taken aback by this breathtaking, history-making aspiration. For a woman in this highly traditional, male-dominated society to reach for formal institutional power has up until now been unheard of. As Kelly Pike, an expert on Lesotho's labor movement and a professor at York University, says, women in Lesotho are "used to living on remittances from their husbands working in South African mines."[39] Now, as they adjust to working in factories, they are also beginning to speak for themselves rather than letting men speak for them. It's certainly not easy. Mampoi told me, "We don't trust ourselves. We are afraid to stand in front of the people speaking English." I pointed out that they were all speaking English and making themselves perfectly understood at that very moment. She laughed. "Now we are speaking perfectly because it's only you. But if it's fifty or thirty people, or it's a workshop, we are so afraid. It's so difficult. That's where the men can get power. We are always quiet and afraid."

. . .

This is what industrialization looks like up close. Something as simple as a factory job is not so simple after all. Zoom in to the possibility of something called mass employment—way in, to the level where you can see the fear in Mampoi's face—and you understand that development occurs in ways that are not straight-forward. We are accustomed to hearing economists describe job creation using such abstract concepts as productivity and compet-itiveness, but workers who go to those jobs and stick with them day after day must solve a range of problems in their lives that their parents could never have imagined. We'll see later on how African governments and institutions are bootstrapping their way through these unexpected problems; but this dynamic is at play on the individual level as well. Faced with strange new situations, people like Mpho, Mopa, Mampoi, and Ahmed swallow their fear and go to work, on the line, but also in many other arenas of their lives.

As women in traditional societies go to work more, express their grievances more, take on more organizational responsibility, and meet more women who are undergoing the same transforma-tions, they are starting to contemplate a future in which they can step out in front of a crowd, in which they can lead and not sim-ply follow. Women speaking out, taking on leadership roles: these things are becoming thinkable in Lesotho, one of a number of possibilities for transformation of the most fundamental sort that are unleashed by factory work. For Mpho, Mopa, Mampoi, and other women in their position, this must feel exhilarating but also at times terrifying. For the men in Lesotho who are being asked to make room for wives and sisters in positions of power, this must feel destabilizing, even dizzying—an upturning of the social orga-nization that has served their society for generations.

Thus, employment of the sort that factories bring is a question not simply of economics, but also of sociology, psychology, poli-tics, values, and power. Factories in developing countries tend to hire workers who are encountering formal employment outside the home for the first time, which unleashes a torrent of change. People will be forced to move, children will be brought up dif-ferently, social norms will shift, power will change hands. There are no guarantees that this will occur smoothly or well—in fact, the lessons of history suggest the opposite. And yet, there is hope mixed in with the worry. People adapt, learn new skills, provide for their families, invent new futures, perhaps find voices they didn't know they had.

I'm reminded of Mopa's description of her fight to get heaters in her factory—a long struggle that spanned her employment there, her being fired by that factory, and her becoming a full-time union organizer negotiating repeatedly with her former employer. She remembers being called into a meeting with the factory's management and being told that after so much uncertainty over so many years, it had happened. It was only heaters, but it was real change, and it was finally here. "You cry for so many years," she said. "Now it happens—*now*." Her laughter rang out with joy and relief.

CHAPTER 6

Two Steps Forward, One Step Back

Stephen Sigei is a young Kenyan who recently graduated from a local vocational training school as a certified mechanic. He has loved machines all his life, tinkering endlessly with gears, old radios, and any other discarded machines he could get his hands on. He has long fingers and the short sentences of someone used to working with his hands. He smiles often when he talks about his work, a wide, winning, gap-toothed grin, even as he looks down shyly at the end of each sentence.

Stephen holds a remarkable distinction: in April 2016, together with two classmates, he exported US$100,000 worth of machine parts from Kenya to China. The three had won the contract in a national industrial skills competition, and they had worked the desk-size lathes and mills at their school for three months to complete the order. As a result, they got to split the profits—roughly $10,000—with their school.[1] Stephen and his classmates are symbols of a new dream taking shape in Africa: that Africans can manufacture products good enough and efficiently enough to sell to the rest of the world. Currently, only 8 percent of Africa's exports to China are manufactured goods, compared with 30 percent of China's exports to Africa.[2] Thus Stephen's accomplishment has earned the attention of top policymakers in Kenya, who were still talking breathlessly about it months later. Onstage at a high-profile gathering of Kenyan and Chinese officials at the Intercontinental, one of the fanciest hotels in Nairobi, Dinah Jerotich Mwinzi, the principal secretary of the Kenyan Ministry of Education, recounted how she beamed as she watched the shipping container holding Stephen's goods leave for China. "I looked at the container with machine spare parts made in Kenya," she said. "It was such a moment of pride. We're used to seeing goods from China, but this time, we are sending a whole container *to* China. We Kenyans exported to China!" she exclaimed, to boisterous applause from the audience.[3]

But Stephen's real dream is even bigger: to have his own factory, producing spare parts for Kenya and beyond. That dream is part of the second possibility that industrialization can bring to Africa: a local capitalist class. However, despite his world-class skills and his share of the $10,000 from his first contract, Stephen has neither enough cash nor the credit to purchase the necessary machines. Whether he can ever become a factory owner will depend not only on hard work and determination—which Stephen has in spades—but also on the relationships he is able to forge with foreign investors. The latter can offer him a partnership or not, look out for his interests or not, believe in him or not. If Chinese investment in Africa is to spawn a generation not only of African workers but also of African industrialists who themselves own the means of production, multiple elements will be required: individual initiative, complementary business arrangements, and ultimately, that most nebulous of ingredients: personal trust.

. . .

Realizing Stephen's dream of becoming a factory owner will no doubt be an uphill battle, but hopefully not as literal of a battle as what he's endured so far. The $100,000 contract he and his classmates won was the prize offered in a competition for the best machining team in Kenya by AVIC International, a Chinese industrial holding company with significant business in East Africa. AVIC brought eighteen machining teams from all over Kenya to Nairobi, where they trained intensively, eight hours a day for more than a month, on giant industrial lathes and milling machines. At the end of the training period, the teams were given technical drawings for four complicated machine parts and a few short hours to make them into reality. They competed on the accuracy with which they could make the parts, with judges evaluating deviations from the drawings down to fractions of a millimeter.

During the monthlong training phase, Stephen quickly emerged as one of the best machinists in the whole field. With two weeks to go before the final contest, he went to a corner store one Friday night to buy credit for his cell phone. Two men approached him, asking for money. He said he had none. The men pulled out knives. He hardly had time to think before they were upon him. One notched three deep slashes in his back. The other cut down from the top of his head, slicing neatly right down the middle of the embroidered logo on his baseball cap. The attacker's next cut opened Stephen's face from his cheekbone to his nose.

Stephen was not about to go down quietly. He wrestled the knife from one attacker. With their victim no longer defenseless, the two men ran. Stephen walked to a clinic with blood streaming down his head and his back and ended up getting six stitches on his face.

The next day, the competition organizers urged him to rest and recover. He stubbornly refused. He was at the lathe machine at 8 a.m., like all the others, and he trained the full day, like all the others.

But that was not the end of his bad luck. During the final competition, with fifteen minutes to go, as he was making the last component, Stephen accidently cut his hand open. The Chinese organizer told him to go see the medic. Instead, Stephen found a water hose, sprayed the blood out of the open wound, and went back to his machine. When time was called, Stephen had just one more cut to make on his fourth and last part. He begged the officials to let him finish. They steadfastly refused, out of fairness to the other contestants.

Even so, Stephen's scores were among the top three in the competition, and they helped catapult his team to the very top. Although he and his teammates brought home the $100,000 contract, he narrowly missed the individual prize: a full scholarship to earn a master's degree in China.

As a result, after literally spilling blood for his triumph, Stephen's troubles are far from over. Since completing and shipping the landmark machine parts order to China, he has been unemployed. "It's my dream that one day, I will have my own lathe machine, producing my own spare parts," he confided.[4] But that dream seems far-fetched at the moment. He doesn't think his school would let him use its lathes and milling machines to fill other orders even if he could get them, and he has no money to buy such expensive equipment on his own. So he has no choice but to look for work as a mechanic at established companies. Stephen's deferred dream is part of the larger promise of manufacturing: that not only will factories bring steady, good-paying jobs, but that ownership of the factories will eventually pass into the hands of locals. As Stephen's story illustrates, that promise won't be easy to realize—it requires skill, determination, money, and sheer guts. Doubtlessly, many will fail, but a few fight on nonetheless.

. . .

The flying geese theory, and historical experience in America, Asia, and Europe, predict that as factories accumulate in a developing country, locals will eventually take over ownership and become the next wave of manufacturing moguls. There is reason to believe that this will happen in Africa as well. Some countries, perhaps most famously Ethiopia, have policies to encourage local ownership in manufacturing. Many government tenders advantage local manufacturers, and financing by country-level development banks is often available only to locals.

In addition, one of a factory's critical tasks is managing its inputs, which drives manufacturers to push for shorter supply chains. Historically, this has led to the creation of a vibrant supplier base everywhere that factories have agglomerated, and although it's still early days, there's no reason to believe that Africa will be an exception. As factories reach critical mass in various African locales, a crop of supplier factories will no doubt arise to serve them.

Local ownership makes sense because it helps not only with the economics of a factory but also with managing its risks. Foreign investors prize local knowledge, which often drives them to find local partners who understand the market and have a network of local relationships. In volatile countries, such partners also help foreign investors navigate political risk. These relationships can be surprisingly long-lived: the Tung family of chapter 2 is still working with the Nigerian partners it entered business with in the 1960s. Both families—Chinese and Nigerian—have their third generation in management now.

But on the ground, as Stephen's story shows, macro predictions can seem overly breezy. Both parties in a potential new partnership find themselves in new situations with imperfect information and sometimes only the faintest idea how to proceed. Obstacles are numerous, and although the theory says that they'll succeed eventually, many fail along the way.

Perhaps nowhere is this two-steps-forward, one-step-back lurching toward local ownership more evident than in Lesotho. Because the clothing industry that dominates Lesotho's economy is only twenty-odd firms strong, it's striking that no fewer than four local firms have tried to enter the industry in recent years.[5] Their stories represent the four outcomes that are possible when locals try to take over: they may fail outright, challenge incumbent foreign players, form a mutually beneficial relationship with the incumbents, or succeed on their own. Their stories illustrate why local ownership is so hard: everyone is missing something. Elites are missing the hard-earned knowledge of the shop floor and the financial pressure to grind it out in a sweaty sewing room for endless hours. Ordinary, non-elite aspirants are missing the capital to grow their businesses or simply to keep themselves afloat while fulfilling a large order, even in such a non-capital-intensive industry as garment making. Nevertheless, new entrepreneurs enter the fray all the time, attesting to the continued allure and enormous—though as yet largely elusive—promise of owning something for oneself.

As in the United States, where half of all entrepreneurial ventures close down within five years, failing at a new business is always a distinct possibility.[6] When I met Chris Mohapi, a genteel, well-mannered Lesothan businessman with graying hair and a well-cut suit, he was in the process of winding down his clothing manufacturing venture. He is a successful businessman and member of Lesotho's elite, friend to some of the country's top officials. A couple of years ago, he and a partner started a clothing firm, hiring 150 workers into the factory. Their business model was to subcontract for the bigger companies in town that regularly had extra work for orders with strict deadlines—much as Mrs. Shen, of chapter 3, does. But less than eighteen months later, Chris was shutting down his factory. He and his partner had run into a multitude of problems, each of which compounded all the others. They had decided to lease machinery from another local clothing firm to save money, and they didn't foresee that it would give them all its oldest and worst machines. The ballooning expense of machine maintenance, along with the downtime it required, drove up their costs alarmingly. On the labor front, they had relied on a much-touted training center supported by the Lesothan government and the World Bank, yet their workers turned out to be less productive than their competitors', who had learned the trade simply by working on the job. The plant's economics required that workers produce 150 garments an hour to break even, but they never achieved better than 120 garments an hour. The downtime caused by the malfunctioning machines and the lower production rate caused by the inefficient workers combined to doom the factory to failure.[7]

One way to overcome the challenges Chris faced is to partner more closely with existing companies. That could make it less risky for locals to enter the clothing business, and allow Asian bosses tired of the grind to quasi-retire but still share in the profits. Mabereng Seiso, a member of the Lesothan royal family who wanted to try her hand at business, entered into such an arrangement with Jennifer Chen, a Taiwanese businesswoman who had for more than two decades run a successful factory in Lesotho that made clothing for well-known international brands such as Old Navy and the Gap. In recent years, Jennifer had become increasingly involved in charity work and wanted to spend more of her time away from the factory. She had become a Lesothan citizen and wanted the business she had painstakingly built to eventually pass on to one of her adopted countrymen. Since the factory was a going concern, she devised an arrangement whereby Mabereng could rent and operate all aspects of it, taking advantage of the well-trained workers, plant processes, and long-term customer relationships that Jennifer had already put in place. Jennifer would get a steady rent for these assets, and Mabereng would keep the profits. It seemed like a foolproof plan: Mabereng could learn the clothing business in a well-functioning, model factory, and Jennifer could step away from the daily grind of the factory floor but watch her life's work continue.

According to Jennifer, it was only six months in when she started suspecting that something was wrong. (Mabereng declined multiple requests for an interview.) Bills for water and electricity were going unpaid, and Mabereng became suspiciously hard to get hold of by phone. A year after the arrangement began, it was clear to both parties that things weren't working out: orders stopped coming in, and Mabereng owed Jennifer increasing amounts of money. Jennifer believes that their arrangement failed because members of the local elite who want to go into manufacturing don't realize that they need to put in arduous, around-the-clock management. "There are more and more rich people in Lesotho, and even fifteen years ago, some of them wanted to get into the manufacturing business," she told me. "But they couldn't withstand the pressure. For example, for us [in Lesotho], there's a time difference with America and with Asia. I'm used to catering to [Asian] business hours, but many of the locals don't. They just say, 'I have to rest now.' "[8] Whatever the reason for the partnership's collapse, Jennifer eventually took back her factory. Disillusioned by her experiment with local ownership, she is now working with a Taiwanese partner. Mabereng has not given up, however: while apparently avoiding Jennifer's debt-collection calls, she obtained a new factory on the other side of town. When I visited, half a dozen workers were setting up a rudimentary production line.[9]

Despite the bitter ending to Mabereng and Jennifer's once-promising relationship, not all arrangements between local and foreign businesses are doomed to failure. Thabiso Mothabeng is living proof that they can flourish. For nearly two decades, Thabiso ran the Mountain Textile Screening Company, which specializes in printing T-shirts and other cotton clothing (think the classic Old Navy T-shirts of the 1990s—his firm printed more than a few of them). In the 1990s, he was the only black factory owner in the Lesotho garment industry, and he had to prove himself to the other owners, who were all Asian. "They didn't believe that a local person would venture into that kind of business," he told me. "It was a matter of convincing them that I could do it. You have to do samples—they give you small orders, and you have to do your best and do them well. At the end of the day, being a local person in an industry that nobody else except you do, in this country, is very difficult." Even after he had proved himself and was regularly taking orders from major customers, it was a lonely life. He describes one meeting with Gap, Inc., during which the Asians clustered on one side of the room speaking Chinese, and the American Gap executives clustered on the other side speaking English. He was the only local, so out of sheer chutzpah, Thabiso started talking to himself in Sesotho.

Nevertheless, Thabiso formed a productive and mutually beneficial partnership with the local Asian clothing firms. They cooperated on the entire process, from generating customer orders to finishing the goods. "I had to work together with the Chinese," he told me. "I went to Asia, namely China, Hong Kong, Singapore, Taipei, just to meet buyers. You have to tell buyers that in Lesotho, there is a printer of this magnitude." He coordinated production with the Asian firms, because his screen printing needed to happen right in the middle of their production processes. "They cut [the cloth], then we print, then we take it back to them to finish it up," he said. And his economics complemented theirs: not every order needed screen printing, so it made sense for a cluster of clothing factories to have only one screen printer rather than having every factory invest in its own screen-printing machinery, skills, and processes. In recent years, Thabiso has seen his business decline as fashions have changed and customers' demand for screen-printed clothes has faded. But his company's nearly two decades of operations is a testament to the fact that local owners can indeed make it in the big leagues: at its height, the Mountain Textile Screening Company printed 20,000 garments a day in ten colors.[10]

If Thabiso is the proud old pioneer who managed to hold his own in a foreign-dominated industry for twenty years, Luqy Adams is the brash youngster dreaming bigger and aiming to go further than any local has before. Luqy is a member of the youngest generation to enter his family's business, which his great-grandfather founded a century ago. A year before I met him, Luqy got himself a spot on a US government–sponsored trip to attend a clothing industry sourcing show in Las Vegas—the sort of forum where big US apparel brands mingle with developing-country factory owners, and deals are cut over a beer and a handshake. Although Luqy had only ever produced small runs of T-shirts and tights with ten-odd workers, he threw caution to the wind and went after a big bid. He was up-front about his company's limited experience, but at least one customer liked his honesty and his ambition. He came home with an order for 2.6 million chiffon tank tops with a glittery appliqué across the front. The order was worth $20 million—not bad for an established company, much less for a rookie like Luqy.

He came home elated by his coup, but then the real work began. From a workshop of ten people, Luqy needed to quickly scale up to four hundred. Beyond the scramble to simply get bodies in the door, Luqy faced the age-old problem of efficiency. Very few of the workers had experienced sewing chiffon—a slippery, tricky material. As a result, they were averaging an output of 350 to 400 pieces a day when they should have been cranking out 500. Furthermore, cash was extremely tight. Clothing industry norms dictate that Luqy be paid only when an order is complete. He must front the money for all the fabric, trim, and other materials. The Lesothan government provided a guarantee for one shipment of materials, but even so, Luqy's cash flow was constantly strained. And because Luqy was scaling up his factory dramatically, he needed to find the money for hundreds of additional sewing machines. He could buy only a few machines at a time, many of them used and mismatched, rather than put in a more efficient single order of standardized models.[11]

Despite these headaches, when I met him, Luqy exuded optimism about his future in the clothing industry. He saw the challenges he faced as growing pains that will fade with time rather than as permanent handicaps. And if he pulled off his audacious feat and completed his $20 million order, he would be in the big leagues. He wouldn't be relegated to subcontractor status, like Chris, or dependent on foreigners, like Mabareng, or stuck in a niche, like Thabiso. He would have customer relationships of his own, and a track record to generate more orders. He would have cash in the bank and no need to buy more machinery, and he would have hundreds of workers with experience with his production system.

Only time will tell whether Luqy pulls off his big order, becoming the biggest success—or the biggest failure—of the bunch. These four local owners—Chris, Mabereng, Thabiso, and Luqy— illustrate the diversity of the locals who aspire to own the means of production. From well-heeled royalty to ordinary small businesspeople, they bring differing skills and shortcomings to their endeavors. The elites are well connected, lacking neither cash nor state backing, but short on factory-floor experience and perhaps naive about whom to trust. The no-name business owners are scrappier and understand the nitty-gritty of the shop floor, but struggle to obtain credit and to generate enough cash to grow. The four also have something in common, however: they're optimistic that locals can do more than make a day wage, and they're up for the challenges and thrills of undertaking long-term risk, competing for orders, and of course, bringing home the spoils. With that mindset, Luqy is scaling a steep and precarious cliff, one that leads to a promised land all four Lesothans believe exists. Even the ones that fall feel the allure of what's at the summit. As Chris wound down his first foray into factory ownership, he was already thinking about his next shot. "The movement has started," he declared. "People are seeing what is possible, and I hope that more of us will get into it and take it forward so that in a couple of years we have ten aspiring local factories. It seems like a natural progression."

· · ·

"A natural progression." That ought to be the case, but some major historical examples show otherwise. For a century, East Africans of Indian descent have dominated the manufacturing sector in Kenya. In fact, the Kenya Association of Manufacturers might as well be called the Indian Kenyan Business Association, given the paucity of any other race in its membership. Despite a century of living in, doing business in, and having children in Kenya, the Indian population in the country is remarkably distinct. Intermarriage between Indian Kenyans and black Kenyans is rare, and an Indian Kenyan factory owner who wants to get out of the business sells as often to Indians in India as to black Kenyans. In West Africa, the Lebanese follow largely the same tradition, resisting local integration despite more than a century of doing business and in many cases raising families there. In Cote d'Ivoire, Lebanese manufacturers have maintained stronger ties to Lebanon and the Lebanese diaspora than to the West African business community. It would be a shame if the Chinese that are appearing in ever larger numbers in Africa took the same course, forming a separate community that in 2100 has stronger ties to China than to Africa.

What is needed for this current wave of Chinese manufacturing to localize in ownership over time? That's the question I had in mind when I went to see Mrs. Zaf Gebretsadik, the African co-owner in one of the most successful African–Chinese collaborations I have encountered.

Mrs. Zaf is a middle-aged Ethiopian with a brilliant white smile and a halo of puffy brown hair. Her coffee-colored skin glows, and her red nails are impeccably manicured. She favors brightly colored blazers and gold jewelry. She likes to press biscuits and Ethiopian tea upon her guests, nudging the platter forward gently like the perfect hostess. But we're not in a living room, and Mrs. Zaf is not some housewife. We're in the conference room of one of the companies she built from the ground up, of which she is the CEO. Starting with a one-person company in 1992, she now owns three companies that employ three hundred people. What's more, she has built her companies in true partnership with

Chinese businesspeople, and those relationships have not only survived but flourished over more than two decades. How have Mrs. Zaf and her Chinese partners made cross-cultural collaboration work whereas generations of Indian Kenyans and Lebanese Ivorians have not? What's her story?

Mrs. Zaf graduated from pharmacy school in Ethiopia in the early 1980s and then worked as a pharmacist in a government hospital. In the mid-1980s, the drought and accompanying famine that made Ethiopia famous all over the world for heart-wrenching images of starving children struck. She joined a relief organization and then transitioned to doing research in pesticides. In 1992, she decided to set up her own company. In her work as an agricultural researcher in a largely agrarian economy, she had seen the need for both human and animal medicines, and she spotted a business opportunity. Ethiopia made very few medicines, so she concluded that more ought to be imported. She knocked on the doors of the Chinese, French, and Swiss embassies. Only the Chinese were responsive. "I went straight to the Chinese embassy, the Economic Consular Office," she laughingly recalled, shaking her head at her own impetuousness. With its help, she managed to connect with multiple Chinese drug manufacturers and became their official representative for the Ethiopian market. Within two years, she was winning big tenders from the Ethiopian government for medical supplies.

A few years later, one of the Chinese companies she represented (and does to this day) came to her with an intriguing proposition: Why not form a joint venture to make gel capsules, the glossy casings that hold drugs?

As is her nature, Mrs. Zaf jumped right in. She put up the capital—basically all her profits to date—for a 30 percent stake in a new company they named Sino-Ethiop Associate Africa PLC. It became the first and only gel capsule manufacturing plant in sub-Saharan Africa. Mrs. Zaf's expertise in the Ethiopian market and her savvy in navigating the Ethiopian bureaucracy were a perfect complement to her two Chinese partners: one specialized in pharmaceutical sales in developing countries, and the other in gel capsule manufacturing technology. The plant was soon up and running and very quickly turned a profit. Initially producing 2 million capsules a day, Sino-Ethiop now makes 6 million a day, with imminent plans to expand to 11 million. This single company accounts for almost all Ethiopia's pharmaceutical exports, and its products are sold all over Africa and the Middle East.[12]

When I visited the plant, in mid-2016, I saw exactly zero Chinese people in the entire facility. Although the plant had been set up and initially run by Chinese technicians, the company quickly transferred skills and responsibility to locals. Ten percent of the Ethiopian staff members were sent to China to be trained in fully functioning gel capsule factories, and as the Ethiopians gained confidence in their abilities, the Chinese workers at Sino-Ethiop went home. Today, all but two of the 170 permanent employees at Sino-Ethiop are Ethiopians. "Now I can say we are experts," Shegaw Aderaw, the deputy general manager of Sino-Ethiop and a proud Ethiopian, told me. "If we want to start a new factory, we can do it by ourselves."

Today, in addition to expanding the factory, Mrs. Zaf has other business ideas. She recently started a pharmaceuticals packaging factory, because even the Styrofoam used to protect the heat-sensitive gel capsules at Sino-Ethiop has had to be imported. She also plans to move into drug production, filling the capsules that Sino-Ethiop makes with active pharmaceutical ingredients. For both new ventures, she will work with Chinese partners. She says of her partners, "I really like them, I trust them, and I get along with them."[13]

All this was made possible by that fateful decision Mrs. Zaf made fifteen years ago. Now that she is a manufacturing mogul, the decision seems obvious, but back then, it really wasn't. It was a big leap for Mrs. Zaf—transitioning from a sales and marketing business that needed very little fixed investment to a manufacturing business with enormous fixed costs. She had to put essentially all her profits to date into a brick-and-mortar factory—a big risk, given that she had never worked in or run a factory before.

But by her own telling, in the end, the decision didn't come down to business considerations. Instead, it was a matter of trust. "I didn't hesitate," she told me. "I wasn't sure if I would make it financially, but I have known these people since 1992. I really trust them. They are like family."[14]

Mrs. Zaf's story points to the magic ingredient that's needed if the Chinese in Africa today are to avoid becoming enclaved communities like the Indian Kenyans and the Lebanese Ivorians. For Africans to increasingly own the means of production, the strivings of local entrepreneurs and the business abilities they possess are only part of the equation. The other part is relationships—whether budding business partners have a true affinity, whether each trusts the other enough to share when a promising new opportunity arises. Here is where business becomes personal: for local ownership to become a reality, local integration must happen first. Will more and more Africans and Chinese form trust-based relationships, the way Mrs. Zaf and her partners did in Ethiopia? Or will Chinese factories become islands in the countries in which they operate? The answer to this question rests upon the answer to another, much deeper one: Will Chinese people start imagining themselves to be part of Africa as well as of China?

The writer Salman Rushdie, one of the foremost chroniclers of the complexities, meanings, and ironies of migration, has described the migrant as someone who sees the world only through a broken mirror, "some of whose fragments have been irretrievably lost."[15] It is out of these fragments, and also of absences, that the migrant must construct something new. And it is in this imperfect, cracked, pieced-together mirror that the migrant must reflect his identity.

Rushdie was dealing in metaphor, but such a mirror indeed exists for Chinese migrants to Africa today. Given the techie tendencies of young Chinese people, it is perhaps not surprising that it's a social media platform. Bobu Feizhou is a virtual space for reflection for Chinese migrants to Africa. It was cobbled together by a young Chinese writer and entrepreneur named Zi Ran. He and his wife had lived in Kenya for six years, having originally come over to work for Xinhua, the official Chinese news agency. As he became more deeply enmeshed in life in Kenya, Zi Ran was increasingly perturbed that no one who wrote about Chinese in Africa understood the worldview or experiences of the Chinese African community of which he was a part. Official Chinese publications, including his employer, printed shallow, glossy accounts of Chinese good deeds. At the other extreme, the African and Western media reported on Chinese migrants with suspicion, covering them only during scandals of one sort or another. Zi Ran saw nothing that represented himself and the people he knew— young, curious Chinese who were trying to make a life for themselves in Africa.

Zi Ran's reaction was to do what most any millennial would do: take to social media. He started a page on the popular Chinese social media app WeChat with a modest mission: to translate and provide commentary on local African news in Mandarin, with an original editorial voice that was both entertaining and informative. The response was overwhelming: not only did readers clamor for more, but people wanted to get involved. Within two months of starting, he had fifty volunteers daily scanning and translating African newspapers. Zi Ran told me about one volunteer who worked long days running a successful business but nonetheless unfailingly stayed up late each night to edit his share of the content. Readership grew, as the Chinese would say, *fan le fan*—it doubled and then doubled again. At work at Xinhua one day, Zi Ran received what in the Chinese system amounted to the ultimate backhanded compliment. He was pulled aside and told in oblique terms that he should quiet down his little WeChat page, because it wouldn't look good for the Chinese government if his side gig outshone its official media platform.[16]

Zi Ran realized that he had unwittingly tapped into a latent but powerful desire within the Chinese community in Africa to reflect honestly about its experiences. Bobu Feizhou meant something to the volunteers who worked on it and the readers who consumed its content because it helped them gather the fragments of their experience and try to mold them into meaning. So instead of backing down, Zi Ran doubled down. He quit his job at Xinhua and struck out on his own. Over the next few months, he and his friends changed the mission of their WeChat page from a news translation site to a space for authentic reflection by ordinary Chinese living in Africa. If the response of their readers to the news site had been impressive, it was now overwhelming. They racked up 100,000 followers in a matter of months. It turned out that many Chinese in Africa felt the way Zi Ran did: jaded by official rhetoric but still desirous of doing good; disgusted by some of their compatriots' actions in Africa but still strongly identifying as Chinese; appreciative of Africa yet not sure about their long-term future there. Reading the site was a way for many to process a life in limbo and perhaps even forge meaning out of their bittersweet lives.

The piece that perhaps best sums up the dilemma of the Chinese African community is an original essay titled "Unable to Remain in Africa, Unable to Go Back to China."[17] At turns funny and heart-wrenching, it describes the minutiae of lives suspended between two worlds yet fully fitting into neither: having friends and relatives in China gradually get busier during the times they're supposed to call you in Africa; being yelled at on an annual trip back to China for paying full price for a movie ticket because one hasn't heard of the latest discount app; being called "uncle" by one's own son after not seeing him for a year. At the heart of the essay is a recognition that Chinese in Africa face a wrenching decision: make a home there, or continue to define home as China from afar. Either way, something is lost: friends, romance, job opportunities, life experiences, a sense of belonging, the dream closest to one's heart. Ultimately, the piece advises its readers that "where your heart is, is home . . . a person, at no point in life, should ever give up on his or her dream."[18]

Zi Ran's mission is fundamentally to forge an identity from the bits of China he brought to Africa and the bits of Africa he is starting to love. It is hard to let go, and it is hard to stay. Building a home is first and foremost an enormous feat of imagination. It requires imagining oneself belonging to a place that feels simultaneously familiar and alien. As Rushdie puts it, "Our identity is at once plural and partial. Sometimes we feel that we straddle two cultures; at other times, that we fall between two stools."[19] It's an "ambiguous and shifting ground," but it's also a creative, "multitudinous," space, one that while shifting is also "hinting at the infinite possibilities" of what could be dreamt into being.[20]

The day after I met Zi Ran for the first time, I met Stephen Sigei, who told me about his dream of owning a machining company, and who was determined to hold on to that dream, despite the odds, and willing to sacrifice for that dream, even to the point of bleeding for it. In more than one way, the dreams of young Chinese like Zi Ran and young Africans like Stephen are intertwined. Will Chinese investors ever see Africa as their true home, and Africans as partners and neighbors in the same shared community? Will young Chinese entrepreneurs like Zi Ran ever get to know African entrepreneurs like Stephen well enough on a personal level to tie their fortunes together and cofound a business? And when foreigners like Jennifer Chen want to get out of the business, will ties of trust and loyalty to an adopted African home drive them to sell to locals rather than to yet more foreigners?

The flying geese theory predicts that somehow, over time, factory ownership will eventually pass on to the receiving country, but the theory is light on the specifics. Up close, this confident prediction often feels less so; but perhaps that is simply the nature of watching history in real time. What is clear, although perhaps unexpected, is that two sorts of audacity will be needed to create a class of local factory owners in Africa. It will take the audacity of sheer grit and bluster and blood, of Africans like Stephen Sigei and Luqy Adams who are dreaming big and taking their shot. But it will also take the audacity of letting go and leaping toward trust, of Chinese like Zi Ran and Mrs. Zaf's business partners who are investing not only their money but also their hearts in Africa. Where these two types of audacity meet is where local integration happens, where local owners take their place alongside Chinese transplants. Because it's not only economics that drives a Chinese factory owner to give a young worker the chance to make it to the top. And it's not only the need for a paycheck that drives a young African mechanic to fight for that chance. It's a human connection, an unspoken feeling, a sense of following a calling, of making a home.

CHAPTER 7

Good (Enough) Governance

Two years ago, I went to Kenya to help create a worker skills training program. My motivation was to see if it was possible for Chinese companies to contribute actively toward good governance in Africa. Many are skeptical: from Hillary Rodham Clinton to my childhood hero, the primatologist Jane Goodall, a wide array of voices have warned of the coming of "a new colonialism in Africa."[1] The worry is that Chinese investment will weaken Africa's institutions, leaving them incapable and irresponsible for generations, much as Western colonialism did. I had researched British colonialism in Kenya for my undergraduate thesis, so these concerns felt both plausible and pressing to me. I wanted to do something to help, so when I found an NGO that was trying to work with Chinese companies in Kenya to help solve local problems, I packed my bags for Nairobi.

In Kenya, I met Isaac Fokuo and Wang Yuan, the unlikely duo who ran the Sino-Africa Centre of Excellence (SACE) Foundation, an organization committed to improving Chinese-African relations. Together, they encapsulated a twin set of concerns about Chinese investment and local governance. Yuan, Chinese herself, worried that Chinese firms might be importing problematic practices: ways of doing business that neglected to build the capacity of local people and corrupted local governments. Isaac had an opposite worry: that poor local governance might weaken Kenya's ability to attract foreign investors, especially from China. As an African who had built multiple successful businesses of his own before starting the SACE Foundation, Isaac firmly believed that the way to sustain prosperity for developing countries was to attract and grow businesses. He was concerned that the Kenyan bureaucracy's lack of responsiveness and the periodic outbursts of violence associated with elections might make investors hesitant to commit to the country, denying it the capital and expertise needed to grow. He pointed to Yuan's in-house research showing that more than half the Chinese companies operating in Kenya identified corruption as a "very significant obstacle" to doing business there. If they are both right, the result is a grim choice: governance without growth, or growth without governance.

We decided to run an experiment of sorts to see if it was possible to break out of this dilemma. We brought Kenyan government agencies, local nonprofits, and major Chinese companies together to work on a problem that everyone agreed needed to be solved: youth development. For local Kenyan stakeholders, youth unemployment—nearly double the rate for the rest of the population—was a pressing social issue that had been spiraling out of control.[2] For Chinese companies, the lack of a skilled local workforce was a major business expense; as a result, they had to bring in technical staff from China, driving up their costs and eroding their profitability. It seemed obvious that all parties—Chinese companies, the Kenyan government, local communities—would benefit from creating a vocational training program for local youths. Yuan and I worked on this project for months, observing vocational schools, visiting job sites, convening decision makers, pestering politicians, and running the numbers. We designed a detailed training program and a rollout plan. Through Yuan's connections with the local Chinese community, we even persuaded AVIC International, a major Chinese construction and heavy equipment company with several major projects in Kenya, to pay for the program and provide the trainers.

But our seemingly unstoppable momentum ground to a halt when we ran into a little-known government agency called the Teachers Service Commission (TSC). We had worked extensively with the Ministry of Education, Science, and Technology and with policymakers from the Kenyan executive branch and the office of Kenya Vision 2030, the national economic development coordinator. But the TSC turned out to be not beholden to any of these other government bodies, and it had autonomy in assigning teachers to vocational colleges. So we could train as many teachers as we liked, but the TSC would almost surely reassign them to other schools. Without knowing where the teachers would go, it was impossible to know where to send students to get the new, better training. And without any assurance that it could hire students with upgraded skills, AVIC International understandably balked at paying for the program and the trainers.

Yuan and I panicked when we hit this roadblock. Indeed, it was a major setback: we had lost months of work, and some of the relationships we had carefully cultivated were no longer useful. We had to go back to the drawing board, which was agonizing after we had come so close and our design made so much sense to everyone other than this pesky little agency.

In my recollections afterward, I identified this as the moment when our project failed. Perhaps because it accorded so strongly with the standard explanation for why promising initiatives in developing countries stall, I blamed "the bureaucracy" and "the lack of institutional capabilities" in Kenya. Only later did I come to understand that these concepts—bureaucracy, institutions—are not static. They evolve, and experienced companies know how to nudge their evolution along, letting their own business models be transformed in the process. In the course of investing on an ambitious scale in Africa, Chinese companies bring with them a powerful assumption: that African governments are good enough for them to do business in Africa. "Good enough" is an assessment that carries risk—a slippery slope that may very well lead to groupthink or corrupt practices. But it is also a space of creative possibility, one that can give rise to social learning and institutional innovation. Development happens not by plan, but by bootstrapping together fixes on the fly. Tentative, uncertain, but hopeful: this is the possibility that "good enough" governance can become good governance, that failure may yet turn into success.

. . .

A year and a half after I left the skills training project in Kenya, I finally called up Qi Lin, a project manager at AVIC International when the company had strongly considered funding our program. During the eighteen months since our project's collapse, we had exchanged occasional greetings on WeChat, the Chinese social media platform, but I had been avoiding a real conversation. I had been deeply disappointed by the failure of our hopeful experiment, and for a while it had seemed to me that my experience in Kenya had proven only my naiveté. I was afraid to talk about it, because it might hammer home the dismal conclusion that Chinese investment really was incompatible with good governance in Africa. But I had started writing this book, and I wanted to confront this important question head-on, so I worked up the courage to ask Lin for a real conversation. Nevertheless, as the phone rang, I half hoped that he wouldn't pick up. But he did, and we ended up talking for two hours.

At the beginning of the conversation, when I asked Lin why he thought our project had failed, his free-wheeling northern Chinese lilt jumped up a decibel. "What do you mean, 'failed'?" he exclaimed. "I don't think that's right. We didn't fail. We almost succeeded!"

I laughed. What was the difference between failing and almost succeeding? Close but no cigar. Second best ain't good enough. Almost doesn't count. Clearly, Lin was just playing with semantics.

But Lin was serious, and he was not amused by my laughter. "What about the NYS?" he asked me. That was a good point, I conceded. The NYS is Kenya's National Youth Service; after we ran into the TSC roadblock, Lin had realized that the NYS was an already functioning worker training institution, and because it was governed by another branch of the bureaucracy, it wasn't subject to TSC rules. We had several promising conversations with its representatives, but I had to return to the United States before any of our talks came to fruition.

"And what about the KTTC?" Lin barreled on. That was another good point. After running into TSC's obstructionist stance, our partners at the Ministry of Education, Science, and Technology had suggested that we work not with a vocational school, but rather with the Kenya Technical Trainers College, which trains vocational teachers. We had a long conversation with Charles Imbali, the KTTC's principal, who was enthusiastic about our idea and added a wonderful twist: to apply learning by doing for teachers as well as for students. Together, we sketched out a model whereby the teachers would learn a technique from a master Chinese trainer and then teach it to students. This was brilliant—a model that produced both trained students and trained teachers.

I was starting to understand Lin's point. "There was also KAM," I piped up. After the TSC stall, the Kenyan vice president's office had asked us to reach out to the Kenya Association of Manufacturers (KAM). When we met with Rajen Shah, the association's chairman, he immediately understood the new business opportunities that computer numerical control and other modern machining techniques would bring to KAM's 800 members, who represent the entirety of Kenya's manufacturing sector. Shah proposed a timeshare model whereby they could lease the advanced machinery and pay for Chinese trainers for their workers. He had wanted to move quickly: he proposed bringing up the idea at the association members' meeting the very next week and running a survey that same week to ascertain precise demand for each type of machinery. I was taken aback—I would be returning to the United States the following day, so I could not meet his aggressive timeline and asked him to push it back. Far from the stereotype that developing country actors move slowly, I was the holdup.

Lin's point was this: the project had almost succeeded because all the endogenous elements were good enough. After we encountered a roadblock, we found that we were dealing with a reflexive, self-regenerative system with actors that could reconfigure into new arrangements to produce novel solutions. When one institution was incompetent and uncooperative, Kenyan stakeholders instinctively started building bridges toward other institutions with the relevant capabilities. When our initial model fell apart, we discovered multiple alternative ways to solve the same problem. And the best part was, we didn't have to come up with the new solutions ourselves—various motivated actors generated new ways of addressing the bottlenecks and added creative ideas to the mix.

There is a term for this process: *bootstrapping development*. Expressed most eloquently by the Columbia University social scientist Charles Sabel, bootstrapping is an understanding of economic development as a process whereby imperfect institutions are able to produce good outcomes by constantly learning about evolving conditions and adapting to them. This is a dynamic, optimistic view of institutions, one that emphasizes less what they are today than what they might become. As Sabel wrote, "If growth-favoring institutions are indeed built by a bootstrapping process where each move suggests the next, then such institutions are as much the outcome as the starting point of development."[3] This theory offers a fascinating interpretation of what happened in the youth development case in Kenya: far from being a permanent setback, the TSC obstacle ignited a learning process whereby the rest of the system reconfigured itself into a more effective model.

Bootstrapping development is a radical idea that bucks how leading thinkers in the West have conceptualized the process of economic development. For more than a century, the prevailing paradigm of what drives the process of economic development has been the "endowment" view—that poor countries must somehow acquire a new, better, "right" set of characteristics in order to grow. What constitutes these "right" characteristics has changed with scholarly fashions through the generations, but the underlying relationship—endowment driving outcomes—has remained constant. In the late nineteenth century, the German sociologist Max Weber asserted that the "right" endowment was a certain worldly mind-set that Protestants had and others did not. In the mid twentieth century, the emphasis was on a state's capacity for large-scale, multiyear planning. More recently, the Washington Consensus emphasized respect for property rights and the rule of law. And to the extent that a view prevails today, the current fashion emphasizes institutions: capable, motivated institutions will drive development outcomes. Whenever we talk in terms of "preconditions for growth"—or, in consulting lingo, "enabling context"—we are slipping into the well-worn groove of the logic that we need to fix developing countries in some fundamental way to unlock their potential.

It's very hard to argue with such a view, in part because it makes intuitive sense. The right mindset, a supportive state, functioning markets, good institutions—these are all lovely things to have, and when we consider countries that have successfully developed, we can see how each had one or more of them in abundance. This seemingly ironclad mental framing has led to a sort of pessimistic intervention in Africa, by Africans and foreigners alike, to create institutions of good governance. It led Tony Blair to create the African Governance Initiative, which sends foreign consultants to work in African ministries, and Mo Ibrahim to create his epon-ymous prize, a monetary award given to African heads of state for stepping down after their appointed term in office. Perhaps the most extreme example is Jeffrey Sachs's Millennium Villages, which literally tries to start everything from scratch, in order to get everything "right."

By contrast, Lin and his employer, AVIC International, exhib-ited a totally different sensibility. They focused on how to make conditions merely "good enough." Perhaps because China itself is a place where government agencies and other institutions are very much under construction, many Chinese companies are undaunted by the prospect of incomplete and evolving institutions. Rather than forming rigid plans, they are comfortable bootstrapping as they go along—pivoting toward various local partners and adjust-ing accordingly. This bootstrapping is accompanied by a mindset at once relentlessly realistic and irrepressibly optimistic. That's what's contained in Lin's assessment that we "almost succeeded": a for-mulation that even while acknowledging our failure thus far, cast the distance between failure and success as imminently bridgeable.

For me, Lin's interpretation opened up a radical possibility. What if there is no linear, straightforward relationship between endowment and outcomes? What if the real story is both more complicated and more hopeful? What if developing countries already have the ingredients they need to start growth? What if what's needed is not the "right" mindset, institutions, or ideas, but instead ones that are merely good enough? And what if the rela-tionship actually works the other way: instead of institutions pro-ducing outcomes, what if it's outcomes that produce institutions?

. . .

Institutions are like muscles: if they're not used, they die. In Nigeria, the customs agency is an institution that everyone had long left for dead. When Transparency International conducted surveys for its

2010 Global Corruption Barometer, it found that more than 50 percent of local households had paid bribes to the customs agency in the previous year.[4] Multiple world-class foreign firms, including Royal Dutch Shell and Siemens, had been involved in corruption scandals involving the customs service.[5] The agency's real function had died, given way to a twisted zombie remnant that fed itself on bribes extracted from almost everyone it dealt with.

In 2006, at the Forum on China-Africa Cooperation, in front of thirty-five African heads of state, the Chinese government announced that it would support six special economic zones (SEZs) in Africa. This was the Chinese government's way of giving back: trying to create in Africa the structures that it believes sparked China's own transformation. Although the worldwide experience of SEZs has been mixed, the ones in China have been spectacularly successful.[6] Stories of the first ones are famous: When my parents went to college, in the early 1980s, Shenzhen was a sleepy fishing village. A mere three decades later, it was the country's fourth-largest city by population and the place where 90 percent of the world's consumer electronics are produced.[7] By financially and operationally supporting African countries in creating their own SEZs, China hoped to translate its own development experience into useful models for others.

The Chinese government found a willing counterpart in Nigeria, so it arranged for the provincial government of Guangdong to support Ogun state in creating the Ogun Guangdong Free Trade Zone. But the Nigeria Customs Service immediately became a headache. Special economic zones are hugely reliant on customs agencies: their proper functioning depends on expedient inspection, paperwork handling, and tariff collection for a constant stream of inbound raw materials and outbound finished goods. The new zone could realize its potential only if basic services such as a customs authority functioned smoothly. Merely calling a plot of land an SEZ wouldn't alter the corrupt practices of the Nigeria Customs Service.

Unfortunately, the first incarnation of the Ogun Guangdong Free Trade Zone did nothing to change the status quo. That is to say, it quickly became a site for rampant smuggling. In 2010, four years after its founding, the zone housed a total of maybe five operational companies—quite a contrast to the grand vision of hundreds of factories humming away. There is some question as to whether the local customs officials corrupted the Chinese zone operator or vice versa, but the end result is undisputable: a haven for illegal activity. One person familiar with the history describes business dealings that routinely involved suitcases stuffed with cash.

Luckily, the Nigerian media noticed. Daily newspapers pointed out that the pace of development was slow and that all kinds of irregularities were occurring while the promised businesses and employment failed to materialize.[8] Under pressure, the Ogun state government sent a warning letter to the SEZ, followed by a letter of termination when matters had not improved.

Meanwhile, in China, two former business executives in their fifties named Jason Han and John Xue were getting bored with early retirement. Jason had run a string of successful factories, and even today, his demeanor suggests the prototypical Chinese factory boss who apparently would rather be making something than saying something. John is as gregarious as Jason is taciturn; one of the few Chinese to obtain an MBA in the United States in the 1970s, he returned to China to help Coca-Cola and then Jack Daniels build their spectacularly successful businesses there.

Jason and John first heard about the Ogun Guangdong zone from the Chinese authorities. They thought it sounded like a good investment opportunity, and the Guangdong provincial government arranged for them to visit. That weeklong trip to Nigeria was their first time in Africa. While they were there, the Ogun state government kicked out the corrupt Chinese management company that had enabled widespread smuggling. In need of new management for the zone, Guangdong officials saw in Jason and John a pair of potential turnaround artists and asked them to take over. Within weeks, the two decided to come out of retirement, move to Nigeria, and run the zone.

One of the most critical tasks Jason and John faced was figuring out how to clean up customs operations. As they describe it, they categorically refused to pay bribes, but they weren't naive: after years of dealing with various petty officials in China to obtain routine permits and other bureaucratic necessities, they knew that they needed to offer some sort of tangible reward for the customs officials in question. But what could they offer that wasn't illegal? Their solution: if not money, then recognition, and the power that comes with recognition for the right reasons. They sat down with the local chief of customs and promised that if he ran a clean operation, they could make the site one of the largest sources of customs revenue in all of Nigeria. With a record like that, he would surely get promoted.

The official agreed. Within three years, the zone had exceeded even Jason and John's expectations. As of 2015, it was generating more than $3 million every month, making it the largest single source of non-oil customs revenue in Nigeria.[9] The official who cleaned up his act and helped make it happen was promoted to the national leadership of the Nigeria Customs Authority. The man who replaced him entertained no thoughts about taking bribes. John laughed as he described it to me: "The customs posting in our zone became a coveted career advancement post! Everybody knows that you go into this post not to play around with funny business but to do things right and get promoted." In a few short years, a significant piece of a formerly decrepit organization had been cured, its culture converted to running on healthy incentives.

As of mid-2016, in the four years under Jason and John's direction, the zone had not only cleaned up the illicit smuggling but also attracted twenty-four legitimate businesses. Collectively, those businesses employed 4,500 people, and all but about 200 were local hires. To better serve the companies within it, the zone set up a 24/7 electricity supply—a rarity in power-strapped Nigeria.

Pause the clock there, and we can glean two lessons. First, no matter how shabby a local institution is, other functioning ones exist as well. In this case, both the local press and the state government tried to hold the Nigeria Customs Service to account and curb its worst excesses. This is the Nigerian version of what Lin pointed out in Kenya: when one local institution becomes a roadblock, there's still hope. No matter how imperfect a developing country institution is, it does not exist in isolation, but rather as a part of a system that can generate its own internal pressures for reform.

Second, institutions don't appear in the world fully formed; rather, they must be used into existence. That is, some firms must be willing to use the institutions in a developing country regardless of how problematic they seem. This is not to excuse the many government officials who take bribes or shirk their responsibilities, or the Chinese companies that feed their worst impulses. And it's an admittedly risky proposition: as the first few years of the Ogun Guangdong zone show, the operator is in very real danger of becoming corrupted by the institution it deals with. But to outright refuse to use country systems is to condemn them to die. Stephen Knack, of the World Bank, and Nicholas Eubank, of Stanford Business School, studied the alternative—that is, when Western donor systems bypass local institutions. They found that "country systems are . . . undermined when donors manage aid through their own separate parallel systems."[10] By creating their own systems, Western donors erode the public's trust in the institutions of the developing country itself. Furthermore, these parallel systems siphon off valuable talent; in Knack and Eubank's words, "When donors bypass country systems they often staff their own parallel aid management systems by 'poaching' the most talented government officials."[11] So although the choice to use imperfect local institutions may resemble risky surgery, not using them is certain death.

Yet risky surgery is just that: risky. The patient could die on the operating table, or appear to be fine, only to suffer from unforeseen side effects later on. The latter is what happened to Jason and John. As of mid-2016, they were riding high: their zone had earned recognition from the Nigerian and Chinese governments for being a shining example of African-Chinese collaboration. A few months later, the state authorities showed up at their doorstep, accusing them of infringing customs and immigration laws and detaining their top manager for fifteen days. No specific allegations were ever produced. Jason and John went into hiding, fearing for their safety. Their assets were seized, and they lost their entire investment in the zone. But according to John, they were lucky: "Given the circumstances, that we were able to leave the country alive is already pretty good."[12]

It's hard to piece together what really happened, but after months of investigation and speaking to various authorities, Jason and John's theory is that the more successful the zone became, the more the management company they had displaced wanted back in. That company still had allies in the Nigerian state government, whom they enlisted to create vague charges as an excuse to kick Jason and John out of the country.

Does this invalidate the premise that developing-country institutions can be used into existence and improved along the way? Is that idea naive? In the aftermath of the Ogun Guangdong disaster, I asked John how he was feeling, and he said, "Optimistic." A man who should be thoroughly jaded regarding the improvement potential of African institutions exuded exactly the opposite mindset. Far from retiring to their comfortable homes in China and ruing their ill-fated Nigerian adventure, Jason and John are already busy planning their next SEZ in Africa. They believe in the ability of African systems to generate solutions, and they believe in their own ability to interact with those systems to produce good outcomes. As John puts it, "For others, resilience is a noun; for us, it's a way of life."[13]

. . .

What makes John so optimistic? Why does he continue to believe that his efforts will pay off, despite all the evidence to the contrary? I think the answer to this is his deep insight that good outcomes are not predicated on the goodness of the actors involved. No ingredient is inherently necessary for success, and highly imperfect systems can produce world-class brilliance.

To illustrate the point, let's look at the clearest case of African success in innovation—mobile payments. M-Pesa is the Kenyan mobile payments platform, and it is unquestionably the most successful system of its kind in the world. Using M-Pesa on their cell phones, Kenyans can send one another money, pay for a wide range of goods and services, and conduct a variety of banking transactions. Because of M-Pesa, mobile payments are much more commonplace in Kenya than in America—in Kenya, even the smallest street vendors are likely to accept M-Pesa. In total, Kenya has 19 million M-Pesa users, who represent about 70 percent of its adult population.[14] More than 40 percent of Kenya's GDP is transacted through M-Pesa, and the number of M-Pesa transactions in Kenya alone outnumbers the number of Western Union transactions in the whole world.[15] Despite the number of powerhouse companies like Google and Apple that have touted their own online payment systems, one out of every two people who send money over a mobile phone is a Kenyan using M-Pesa—an astonishing proportion when one considers that Kenya represents 0.0006 percent of the world's population.[16]

How did Kenyans figure out something that has eluded the rest of the world? There are two prevailing narratives typically told about M-Pesa's origins. One is the Disney version that many Kenyans would like to believe: a scrappy young Kenyan inventor noticed a need and figured out how to fill it through sheer ingenuity. Several lawsuits have been brought by Kenyans who claim to have invented M-Pesa, and perhaps because Kenyans would like to believe that M-Pesa was their doing, the story lives on, even if no one is certain who actually invented it. Dr. Shem Ochuodho, a member of the Kenyan parliament, represented many Kenyans' hopes when he declared, "[T]he true unsung hero [is] the young university student who 'invented' mpesa—the inventor/innovator!"[17]

The other narrative resembles the sort of depressing documentary played at hipster film screenings, showing that large corporations and colonial influences secretly run the world. In this version, a British company invented the quintessential Kenyan innovation with the help of the British government, Kenya's former colonizer. This account does have some basis in fact: Vodafone is a multinational mobile phone company based in the UK, and in 2003, its social enterprises office created a proposal to use mobile phones for delivering financial services.[18] Vodafone applied for and received a million pounds from the British government to develop the idea and pilot its introduction through Safaricom, its subsidiary in Kenya.

As is usually the case, the real story is probably somewhere between a Disney film and a depressing documentary. Sure, Vodacom had a promising idea, but it was not viable in its original form; and M-Pesa would not have taken off to become a global sensation if a variety of Kenyan actors and institutions had not pulled and pushed and reshaped it. In fact, Vodafone's idea was not to serve consumers at all: it initially targeted microfinance institutions—the often social-minded, banklike organizations that make small loans in developing countries—as its core users. Only when Vodafone ran a pilot and observed Kenyans twisting their intended service into new forms—businesses paying one another with it, using it as a virtual cash register for safety during journeys—did the company realize the potential for a mass customer base.[19]

Along with the innovative behavior of individual Kenyan business owners, the imprint of Kenyan institutions made the difference between M-Pesa's success and failure. When I spoke to Michael Joseph, Safaricom's CEO at the time of M-Pesa's rollout, he was unequivocal about how critical the Kenyan government's role had been. Literally the first thing he said to me was "We could not do this without the government's support, both from a political and a regulatory point of view—we could *not* have done this."[20]

Indeed, government after government around the world had been reluctant to support mobile payment systems, and initially, it appeared that Kenya would be no exception. At the time of M-Pesa's pilot, the Central Bank of Kenya had an acting governor who balked at making such a controversial decision. The whole bureaucracy stalled on the M-Pesa question, but one man was determined to make it move: Dr. Bitange Ndemo, the permanent secretary in the Ministry of Information and Communication. Because he came from academia and figured he could return to teaching if things went badly in government, he decided to take a risk. He went straight to the top, personally calling on Mwai Kibaki, the president of Kenya at the time, to explain the model. Dr. Ndemo recalls the crucial moment when Kibaki asked, "What is the benefit?" To which he answered, "It would get the money out from under everybody's mattresses."[21] There was a brief silence as Kibaki considered it. Then the president gave his go-ahead, and the rest is history.

When Dr. Ndemo told me this story, I was taken aback. This was before M-Pesa's rollout—how could he be sure that the system was a good one? What if consumers lost money, and livelihoods were destroyed? "Innovation precedes regulation," he insisted by way of reply. He likened the process of economic development to that of child development: as children learn, they inevitably break a few things along the way. He's not afraid to let firms experiment, and he's not afraid of a few broken toys. In his view, not until he sees how the toys are being broken can he design the right safety mechanisms into regulatory policies. To do so beforehand would be to act like an overbearing parent, afraid to let a toddler learn to walk for fear of a scraped knee. Mistakes are data that aid learning. "Every mistake we make, we learn from," he insisted. "We *must* allow ourselves to learn from our mistakes."

Along with Dr. Ndemo, others in Kenya's bureaucracy acted with courage. Critically, during M-Pesa's early days, the Central Bank of Kenya determined that Safaricom was not acting like a bank and decided not to subject M-Pesa to banking regulations. This was not laziness—the central bank in fact held a long legal review before arriving at its decision—but rather, an act of regulatory wisdom. In what Michael Klein, a former vice president of private sector development at the World Bank, called a "test and learn" approach to regulations, the central bank consciously refrained from creating restrictive rules for mobile payments while the innovation was in its infant stages.[22] Instead, it worked to ensure that a basic safety net was in place to protect consumers, commissioning an extensive operational risk audit to confirm the system's handling of confidential customer data, security features, and ability to report every transaction.[23] When I spoke to Njuguna Ndung'u, the governor of the Central Bank of Kenya at the time of M-Pesa's launch, he summarized his approach as basically "allowing the market to work . . . develop the market but make sure that you assess the risk and deal with emerging vulnerabilities."[24] And crucially, Safaricom was able to use another Kenyan institution that not even the United States has: national ID cards. This allowed M-Pesa to register users and prevent money laundering with a minimum of fuss. But beyond customer safety, the Kenyan regulators declined to require the same level of safeguards for

M-Pesa that banks have. Mukhisa Kituyi, the Kenyan who currently serves as secretary-general of the United Nations Conference on Trade and Development, says, "At the Central Bank, Prof Ndung'u had the audacity not only to ignore the deafening scaremongering of the big banks, and skepticism among high government people, but to stake out that facilitative regulation sometimes entails allowing innovations to go ahead even when the law for regulating it is not yet in place."[25]

If this sounds familiar—waiting and seeing, being willing to experiment, making up the regulations as you go along—that's because it is. The real story of M-Pesa is not only about individual innovation, not only about firm-level innovation, but also about institutional innovation. It is the result of all those levels interacting, setting productive constraints, and seeding new ideas as they go along. This is how development happens—not planned and strategized at the outset by some aid program, but self-generated and pivoting unpredictably at every turn. No single Kenyan could have imagined at the outset what M-Pesa would become; history shows that Vodacom's original idea is not the one that allowed M-Pesa to take off; and Kenyan regulators certainly could not have created M-Pesa by themselves. It is the bootstrapped product of their interacting, which changed the product, the firms, and the laws involved as they went. None of the actors, companies, or institutions involved were perfect, but they were good enough—good enough to create the best mobile payment system in the world.

It's worth nothing that in another realm—namely, American business—this strategy is termed *pivoting* and is so widely accepted that it is part of the required curriculum for Harvard MBA students. Although this flexible, reactive way of doing business has been enshrined as gospel in Silicon Valley, it is still viewed with suspicion in developing countries. There, development institutions still emphasize creating anticipatory strategies from the outset and carefully planning their execution.

Part of the reason for this is that people tend to be much more clearheaded when reflecting on history than when making history. It's a hallmark of successful development stories that people look back on them and see their institutions acting deliberately and in just the right way, whereas playing the story forward in history, no one at the time seemed at all sure of what they were doing and were merely trying to make things good enough to get by. China is a prominent example: as the Harvard Kennedy School professor and China scholar Tony Saich puts it, China has largely been "muddling through." According to Saich, the difference between the centrally planned economy of China and that of the failed Soviet Union is that the Chinese government "has shown a remarkable capacity to adapt to the rapidly changing environment" and that there has been "substantial adaptation of institutions."[26] From reforms allowing farmers to sell excess production to special economic zones, the innovations that are now synonymous with the Chinese economic model were originally kooky one-off experiments in far-flung townships. Saich writes, "Contrary to much press reporting and general perceptions, the political centre does not control the system throughout and there is significant deviation from central policy across bureaucracies and at the local level."[27] Only after China's remarkable rise—the fastest growth any country has ever undertaken—did people look back and think that the government must have known what it was doing all along.

And it's not just China. Many Western countries have used the same approach, to great effect. Small European states such as Austria and Belgium were poor in the period following World War II, with roughly half the per capita GDP of the United States. They adopted an adaptive, bootstrapping approach to working with firms and unions. As the political scientist Peter Katzenstein puts it, "the small European states continually improvise," with economic development strategies that are "flexible, reactive, and incremental."[28] By 1982, those states had both a greater per capita GDP and a higher standard of living than the United States.[29]

It is tempting to look at a country like Austria and believe that it was somehow afflicted with fewer problems than Kenya, which has been plagued by persistent ethnic tension and a convulsive bout of election violence in 2007. We forget that after World War II, the victorious Allies believed that Austria was so rabidly racist and untrustworthy that they banned it from building a domestic car industry.[30] The United States was particularly wary that if they were allowed to have car factories, the Austrians might turn them into bomb factories and start another war.[31] No other country got this treatment—not even Italy, with its remnants of Mussolini's fascism, or Germany, with its remnants of Hitler's Nazism. Only now, looking back after Austria has been prosperous and peaceful for two generations, do we believe its essential character to be the idyllic raindrops-on-roses Alpine gentleness of *The Sound of Music*. Someday, when Africa is prosperous and peaceful and has been that way for generations, we will tell the same sort of happy myths about Kenya and Nigeria.

. . .

One chilly evening in Nairobi in 2016, men and women in power suits—people from the government and business elites of Kenya—posed for photographers with colorful placards saying "Made in Kenya." They nibbled on hors d'oeuvres and exchanged business cards before settling into their seats inside a glitzy ballroom. The Chinese ambassador to Kenya and the Kenyan secretary for education sat in the front row. A line of photographers and cameramen occupied the center aisle. Their lenses were trained on a pedestal covered with a crimson cloth. The Chinese man who headed AVIC International's Kenya business and the Kenyan woman who was the Kenyan Ministry of Education's top bureaucrat stood in front of a backdrop that exhorted, "Dream and Invent Your Future."

Together they gave the cloth a tug, unveiling what was underneath: a plaque memorializing the creation of the Sino-Africa Industrial Skill Upgrading Center.[32] A fancy, formal, unwieldy name for a simple concept: a youth development center.

Two years after I prematurely admitted defeat on our youth development project, I was proven very wrong. Long after I gave up on getting Kenyan institutions to support our project, AVIC International, the Chinese company that we had roped into the project, kept doggedly pushing for new ways of training workers. Of the various leads that emerged after the TSC setback, the Kenya Technical Trainers College idea proved workable. With the support of the Ministry of Education, AVIC decided to partner with Kenya's main vocational teacher training institution, overhauling its equipment and revamping its curriculum.

For AVIC, this was not charity: it was business imperatives leading to social good. When I sat down with Qian Rong, the head of AVIC's Kenya business, he gave two rationales for his company's persistent involvement in technical education: "One, China has a competitive advantage in technical education. This is what changed China itself from an agricultural society to a manufacturing society. Two, bringing that here is good for our company's long-term profit, in addition to resulting in enormous impact on Africa."[33] That classic Chinese businessman's attitude: it's nice that there's impact for Africa, but making institutions in Africa work better is really just good business. It's not warm and fuzzy, but it occurred to me that the youth development center had a better shot at enduring precisely because of that hard-nosed practicality.

Whatever the motivations, the training center had finally come to be. Despite my pessimism, AVIC International managers and their counterparts at the Kenyan Ministry of Education had remained optimistic. Despite my dead-end view of the situation, they had seen it in a creative, flexible way. Perhaps because Chinese firms are fresh from cocreating many institutions essential for a modern capitalist economy in China itself, companies like AVIC International have an instinctive patience and optimism in their approach to developing-country institutions. These companies demonstrate that it's possible to work with African institutions as they are, to innovate together to produce outcomes they stubbornly believe are possible. And more often than one might expect, local institutions rise to the challenge. Failure is not final. A setback begets another experiment. And being told no is just the start of another conversation.

CHAPTER 8

"If We Could Do It, Then So Can This Place"

Sonia was a stick-thin fourteen-year-old girl.* She lived in a dry, sandy, long-impoverished region in Namibia, a country in south-west Africa. She wore her hair in braids.

Sonia was one of my students when I was a public secondary school teacher in rural Namibia. When she needed to get my attention, she would look at me for a long moment and smile a wide, toothy smile before addressing me. "Miss Sun," she would say, in a voice barely above a whisper. When she giggled, she covered her mouth with the back of her hand. She was not my best student, but she was far from the worst. She tried hard, and sometimes when the homework I gave her class was extra difficult, she would knock softly on my door after school and ask shyly if I could explain the lesson again.

I was teaching Sonia's class one day when the principal came in. His big frame filled the doorway, darkening the chalkboard where I was writing. I was alarmed—he rarely left his office during the school day. I stepped out into the school courtyard with him.

*Name changed to protect privacy.

Sonia's mom had died.

My mind simultaneously became very clear and very hazy. I remember explicitly willing myself to walk back into the classroom, to bend down, to gently ask her to come outside. But I can't remember which of us actually said the words a few seconds later. She didn't cry.

Someone had to take her home. The principal couldn't leave the grounds during the school day, so I led her to my car and drove the long, winding sandy roads to her house.

No one ever told me what Sonia's mother had died of. In northern Namibia, this almost always means the death was HIV/AIDS-related. In our village of 500-odd people, a funeral was held almost every weekend. The doctor at the local hospital told me that he thought the HIV infection rate in this region of Namibia was 40 percent. Continent-wide, Africa has 70 percent of the world's HIV patients and 88 percent of its HIV-positive children.[1] Africa also has by far the highest rates in the world of a host of treatable diseases that belong more to the nineteenth century than to the twenty-first. Seventy-nine percent of the world's TB cases and 90 percent of its malaria cases occur in Africa.[2] Africa has half of the world's preventable deaths among children under five years old, and more than half of the world's deaths of expectant mothers.[3] Each year, 300,000 African children die of diarrhea for want of simple rehydrating salts dissolved in clean water, and 473,000 die of pneumonia for want of basic antibiotics.[4] I think about the fact that behind every one of these statistics are countless Sonias, and it's clear that Africa's public health crisis is an unconscionable blight upon the world.

That awful day, as we drove toward Sonia's house, we began to hear the unearthly wails of mourning women long before we got to the entrance. Her aunts, cousins, and neighbors had gathered outside the scattering of huts, sitting on the bare ground. The women were singing traditional songs and crying—a meandering paean of grief. Sonia and I found a shaded spot under a tree and sat down. She finally cried. I cried too as I held her. There was nothing else to do.

That feeling of being so close yet so useless in the face of such senseless suffering is one that has haunted my life and career since. This is not to cast Africa into the tired and untrue stereotype of a "hopeless continent" marred by poverty and disease. Rather, it's to recognize that Africa has many sides, and this—the Africa of children who lose their mothers to diseases the world already knows how to treat—is still unfortunately one of them. Any book that deals seriously with Africa's future must grapple with this reality. A full assessment of the impact on Africa of Chinese investment cannot ignore the continent's human and social needs. The question of what possibilities that investment opens up should be asked not only about workers, local businesses, and governments, but also about the poor, the sick, and the vulnerable. What are the development consequences of Chinese investment in Africa? How has the world treated families like Sonia's in the past, and what would be different if Chinese firms helped the continent industrialize?

. . .

For the past generation, the global response to cases like Sonia's and communities like the northern Namibian one I lived in has been to treat them as one giant emergency: HIV, malaria, and other diseases are a scourge on humanity; we need to stop their spread as soon as possible, before more mothers die and more Sonias are orphaned. In this spirit, starting in the 1990s, a remarkable coalition of Western governments and philanthropists put infectious disease in the poorest regions of the world at the top of the global agenda. The initiative is best exemplified by the Millennium Development Goals—global aspirations assembled by the United Nations in 2000 that for the first time put social services such as health care and education ahead of more-traditional priorities such as spurring foreign investment and providing infrastructure on the development agenda. The sense was that debates about industrial policy and tariff levels were not just arcane but actually immoral in an era in which babies were dying from HIV in large numbers. Saving innocent people's lives—what could possibly be a more obvious priority? To donor agencies such as USAID in America and the UK's Department for International Development, and to powerful new philanthropic organizations such as the Gates Foundation, Africa's public health crisis was declared an emergency not only for Africa but for the whole world. No longer would hapless developing-country governments be allowed to fritter away the foreign aid they received on half-baked economic growth plans. While mothers and children were dying in their countries for want of simple medical care, helping them should be paramount.

These organizations reorganized and reinvigorated a tired global development apparatus. They raised record amounts of money to buy essential medicines and vaccines and formed a crop of new organizations to administer the funds. The Global Fund channeled more than $30 billion into fighting AIDS, tuberculosis, and malaria, and GAVI, The Vaccine Alliance, put another $7 billion into vaccinating children in developing countries.[5] Perhaps most notable is the mammoth $63 billion President's Emergency Plan for AIDS Relief (PEPFAR). Formed under President George W. Bush and extended under President Barack Obama, PEPFAR is the largest health care initiative dedicated to a single disease in the history of the world.[6] Global health resources were amassed in the coffers of these Goliath global programs and administered out of head offices in Europe and the United States, as the funding and decision-making authority of developing countries' ministries of health and drug regulatory agencies became punier and punier by comparison.

The primary interest of this powerful coalition of Western governments and philanthropists is a noble one: to save as many lives as possible, as quickly as possible. Although health outcomes have a number of determinants, including access to care, general infrastructure, educational levels, and social and cultural attitudes, it was undeniable that many developing countries needed more and better medicines. One obvious strategy for acquiring large volumes of pharmaceutical products quickly and cheaply would be to buy from big established factories elsewhere in the world—India being a prime source—which could offer the lowest price per unit for a host of needed medicines, including antiretrovirals, the drugs used in HIV treatment. The global health organizations contracted to buy from these low-cost plants, and in some cases even committed to buying future supplies. This was clever: guarantees of future demand allowed pharmaceutical firms to invest in expanding their factories, further dropping per-unit prices. In a win-win, the pharmaceutical firms could make more money, and the health organizations could treat more patients with the same amount of funding. In large part owing to efforts like these, the price of a year's worth of HIV treatment per patient dropped from $10,000 in 1987 to about $150 in low-income countries today.[7]

These drug-buying programs were just one aspect of the most coordinated and disciplined aid program in the history of the world. On every dimension, the global organizations were a model of rational action: they got together, studied the problem, decided the logical things to do, determined who would do what, and monitored the results. They did studies on how many people needed treatment and calculated how much that would cost, and they got spokespeople from Bill Clinton to Bono to help raise money and awareness. They made plans for countries that laid out what local governments should be doing to eliminate infectious diseases, and they kept global scorecards that effectively graded countries on their performance against the plan. They set ambitious targets for reducing the number of deaths from major diseases, and they single-mindedly held everyone to account for achieving those goals.

It worked. This emergency-oriented, save-lives-now approach did exactly what it was supposed to. Over the past twenty years, new HIV infections have fallen by 35 percent, and HIV-related deaths have fallen by 41 percent. Eighty-three countries have halted or reversed their HIV-AIDS epidemics.[8] From 2000 to 2013, global treatment efforts have saved 37 million people from dying of tuberculosis.[9] The number of childhood deaths has been cut in half, and maternal deaths have dropped by 45 percent—both enormous accomplishments in the context of a burgeoning world population.[10] These are incredible numbers, and ones to be proud of. The human impact is immeasurable: it stuns me to contemplate how many children did not have to go through what Sonia did as a result. I think back to that awful day, and I'm grateful that although these efforts could not change what happened to Sonia, they did reach other families. As former US Secretary of State John Kerry put it, the global health community's work over the past two decades "represents in truth a victory for the human spirit."[11]

. . .

Did this victory have a price? And if so, who is paying it? The question needs to be asked, not to diminish this enormous accomplishment but to make it a lasting one. Only if we understand the price of this victory, and who is bearing its burden, can we understand how long it is likely to hold and how we might make it permanent.

The clear loser in the current global health approach toward Africa is Africa's pharmaceutical industry. This is ironic: although they operate on the continent with the largest market demand for antiretrovirals and a host of other drugs, pharmaceutical companies in Africa are for the most part small and teetering on the verge of collapse. Ethiopia, a country of 100 million people, has nine pharmaceutical manufacturers. By contrast, Germany, population 81 million, has nearly a thousand.[12] And the manufacturers that do exist in Ethiopia are of poor quality: a 2015 evaluation of eight of the nine local producers found that only two met global standards for good manufacturing practice, and none of them produce any products certified by the World Health Organization as pre-qualified for high quality. On a 100-point scale, with 100 denoting "fully meets global quality standards," six of eight manufacturers scored 50 or lower.[13]

The situation is no better across the rest of the continent. With the exception of middle-income South Africa, few African countries have more than a handful of pharmaceutical manufacturers, and the ones that exist are, like Ethiopia's, largely of poor quality. Kenya is the pharmaceutical industry's undisputed standard-bearer in East Africa, yet it has only about forty manufacturers. Most of them are small and inefficient, and only one has met WHO standards for good manufacturing quality. In Tanzania, the local pharmaceutical industry has actually shrunk over the past decade: a WHO study found that of a basket of common medicines, 33 percent were manufactured locally in 2006, but only 12 percent by 2012.[14] In West Africa, Nigeria has the largest concentration of drug manufacturers, with about forty firms, but as in the rest of Africa, they are small, inefficient, and of low quality: currently, none meet global standards for quality manufacturing.

What's more, these local manufacturers are small and substandard as a direct consequence of the way the global health apparatus has decided to deal with public health problems in Africa. By doing the logical thing to save as many lives as possible—buying drugs from India at the lowest rates available—it trapped African drugmakers in a state of perpetual infancy. Because they are small, they have higher per-unit costs, so donors don't buy from them. And because donors don't buy from them—and have flooded their home markets with imports from abroad—they cannot justify scaling up their factories, which would lower their per-unit costs. In their pursuit of a noble goal, the donors doomed African pharmaceutical manufacturers.

This realization is difficult, and uncomfortable to contemplate. We want simple stories, with pure heroes and pure villains, and our minds rebel at the notion of bad outcomes arising from good deeds. This is not a simple story. Both the goodness and the fallout are real. Global health efforts in Africa over the past generation have truly been "a victory for the human spirit" in the rapidity and purposefulness with which they alleviated terrible human suffering. Yet they have unwittingly destroyed a market and crippled an industry in Africa that should be thriving.

The stunting of Africa's pharmaceutical industry has if not other costs, then certainly other risks. For one, disease is neither static nor evenly distributed. It is constantly evolving, mutating to attack the human body in novel ways. When the Ebola virus suddenly appeared on the scene in West Africa in 2014, there was no hope of a vaccine or a cure anytime soon. None of the countries with major Ebola outbreaks had a pharmaceutical industry of their own to speak of, so they had to rely on foreign drugmakers to come up with something fast. In the panic that followed, multinational pharmaceutical companies were roundly criticized for their long neglect of diseases that primarily affect developing countries.[15] But as long as Africa relies on foreign companies for drugs, there will be a shortfall in how much research its diseases get and how quickly any new disease outbreak can be dealt with. The current global health approach of contracting for large volumes of drugs to lower costs has worked well for diseases we know about, but it's useless for those that have yet to appear on the scene. And without African firms that do R&D on African soil, African patients will continue to get the dregs of foreign pharmaceutical companies' research programs.

Furthermore, there is a limit to what outsiders, however well intentioned, can be expected to do. In a phenomenon known in the aid world as donor fatigue, Western governments and taxpayers are increasingly wary of continuing to foot the bill for African health problems. A detailed study by Doctors Without Borders found that the US President's Emergency Plan for AIDS Relief, the World Bank, and UN agencies had all decided to cap, reduce, or withdraw their spending for HIV treatment.[16] In some ways, that's an understandable consequence of the way HIV and other health crises in Africa were framed for funders and the public in the West: this is an emergency, so drop everything and sprint over as fast as possible to help. Now, nearly two decades later, the sprint has turned into a marathon. Even without the economic strain inflicted by the Great Recession, it's hardly surprising that fatigue has set in when a bill that was supposed to occur one time continues to arrive year after year. At the same time that the resolve needed in the West to prop up the global health apparatus is atrophying, the way that global health is being run has weakened the African health care industry and left it in no position to take over once the donors leave.

Even some major donors are having second thoughts about the model they themselves built. "On a high level, the thinking is changing," Daniel Berman, of the World Health Organization, told me. "For example, the Global Fund realizes that this system of insisting on the lowest price and procurement on a global level has its limits. If you want to transition from donor-funded health programs to nationally funded health programs, it really makes a difference to have local manufacturers. Getting a government behind health care priorities is greatly enhanced by having local industries."[17] In other words, unless we assume that all the lives that need to be saved in Africa can and should be saved indefinitely by do-gooders from the outside, local drug industries must exist and thrive in Africa. Far from being an emergency for which all other priorities should be cast aside, saving lives turns out to be intertwined with the African economy in general and local manufacturing specifically.

. . .

At Harvard Kennedy School, there is a puzzle presented in the ethics class required for first-year master's degree students: "Suppose you walk by a pond, and you see that a child is drowning. But it's a really busy day—you have lots to do. Do you have to stop and help the child?"

The answer is obvious. Faced with an emergency of this gravity, to not stop and do everything in your power to save a life would be a moral failure of the worst sort.

"But suppose you walk by a pond every day, and *every day* there's a drowning child," the puzzle continues. "And you're still really busy. Is it unethical to not stop and help the child *every day*?"

This is where the puzzle gets hard. Part of the essential nature of emergencies is that they occur infrequently—that's what distinguishes them from unpleasant facts of life. Yet at what point does an unconscionable situation occur so frequently and so predictably that it forces us to consider it a regular feature of life, subject to the same laws of economics and politics as any other sphere? At a certain point, we need to reclassify: this is not an emergency—it's a structural injustice. Emergencies require a narrow focus—drop everything and take care of this now—but structural problems require holistic inquiry. The solution is not to mindlessly jump into the pond every day to rescue the child but to examine the social and economic forces that lead to this recurrent problem and determine what other social and economic forces might be brought to bear to solve it on an ongoing basis. The question is not "Should I jump in?" but, rather, "How is it that a child is in that pond every day? Who or what led to this situation? Could the kids be taught to swim?"

These questions are not easy to countenance, much less to consider deeply. Yet they are questions that Africans—and the well-meaning global development apparatus—need to face squarely if they are serious about raising living standards and changing life trajectories on the poorest continent in the world. And history suggests that there is another way to approach public health problems: Not as emergencies, but as urgencies. Not as charity, but as industry. Not in a way that distorts local markets, but in a way that develops them.

China and India are two prominent examples. A generation ago, when China was poorer than many African countries, the government offered cheap land and tax incentives to nurture local pharmaceutical firms. As a result, between 1980 and 1999 the number of firms grew nearly tenfold, from 680 to 6,357.[18] In 1947, at the time of independence in India, 80–90 percent of the drugs it used were made by Western multinationals.[19] By the early 2000s, this share had flipped completely: 90 percent of the drugs used in India are now made domestically.[20]

Strikingly, both countries rejected the seemingly irreproachable imperative to save as many lives as possible as quickly as possible. Instead of focusing on public health goals alone, China and India sought to balance a variety of social and economic goals. For China, job creation and the health of local industries were major priorities. Investment in its pharmaceutical firms has often been driven by provincial and local governments eager to get their slice of an industry that grew at double-digit rates for two decades.[21] Implicit in the system was a tolerance for poor quality, with regulations that for years were laxer than global standards for good manufacturing practice and sometimes weak enforcement of the standards that did exist.[22] Only much later, when Chinese firms were well established, did the government begin raising quality requirements as part of an effort to force industry consolidation and encourage innovation. The government could have used the logic of Western donors in Africa, importing cheaper and higher-quality drugs from abroad to save more lives. But it did not, because its aim was to provide jobs and nurture domestic markets as well as to save lives. This was also a short-term versus long-term trade-off: although a domestic industry may mean more lives lost while it finds its footing, it may also mean more lives saved when it matures.

For India, supporting domestic industry is on par with saving lives. In 1970, India passed a patent law that recognized processes rather than the actual substance of drugs, essentially allowing companies to reverse-engineer patented drugs and manufacture them as long as they used a different chemical synthesis process. Foreign drugmakers understandably backed out of the country, depriving India of many new and innovative drugs. But as a result, domestic firms conquered the market and in so doing learned how to become among the most efficient generic pharmaceutical makers in the world.[23] India eventually gave up its process patent law in order to join the World Trade Organization, but to this day, the Indian government uses compulsory licensing and other regulatory measures to keep multinational competition from encroaching on its domestic firms.[24] And it has tended to hold off introducing life-saving vaccines made by foreign firms until Indian drugmakers have figured out how to produce the vaccines themselves.[25] Presented with the option to save lives now at the cost of closing off a part of the health care market to its local firms, the Indian government has consistently declined, choosing to encourage its domestic industry in the hopes of saving lives later.

These are gut-wrenching trade-offs. We have to recognize that China's and India's policies caused people to die in the near term because medicines were expensive, unsafe, or unavailable. But it is also true that wherever factories have appeared en masse, they have unleashed new possibilities—new jobs, new sources of wealth, new societal structures. We in the United States have largely forgotten the experience of development, the fact that it necessitates terrible trade-offs like these. We want feel-good development. But up close, in the moment, the choices are ugly and often heartbreaking. Every country that has industrialized has made choices it would rather not think about. It has also experienced growing pains—labor violations, safety scandals, environmental degradation. But every country that has industrialized has also seen its life expectancy jump noticeably upward and stay there. And after all, isn't giving people longer lives the entire point of public health?

. . .

Today, a few intrepid African countries are trying to refashion their approach to unite health care and industrial development. They are starting to assert the primacy of their local pharmaceutical industries as a major national priority. South Africa, the country with the largest HIV-positive population in the world, is seriously exploring manufacturing active pharmaceutical ingredients for HIV/AIDS medications in order to reduce its reliance on foreign suppliers, which has led in the past to periodic shortages of needed drugs.[26] Kenya, already the leader in pharmaceutical manufacturing in East Africa, has been working on a national plan to encourage additional domestic production.[27]

But nowhere is the push to create a domestic pharmaceutical industry more prominent than in Ethiopia, the second most populous country in Africa, which currently imports 80 percent of the drugs it uses. This is not only a major problem in terms of access to essential medicines but also a major drain on foreign currency reserves.[28] In July 2015, the Ethiopian government unveiled a high-profile national strategy aimed at rapidly developing a robust domestic pharmaceutical sector. The event was meant to make a splash: it was announced by the country's deputy prime minister and attended by multiple government ministers, along with foreign dignitaries such as the chairperson of the African Union and the director general of the World Health Organization.[29] In front of this powerful audience, the Ethiopian government set the ambitious goal of increasing the share of domestic production of the drugs that Ethiopia uses from 20 percent to 60 percent within five years.[30] Significantly, the government abandoned the artificial separation of health goals from industrial development that the global development apparatus has implicitly observed over the past two decades. Instead, Ethiopia explicitly "aligns the objectives of health policy with those of industrial development policy."[31] As Ethiopia's minister of health pointed out, local manufacturing will be equally good for the local economy and for health: it will enhance access to essential medicines and develop local capacity to generate solutions for local health problems.

To be clear, this will be hard. It's one thing to proclaim in a glossy pamphlet what is possible; it's another to make it actually happen. This became apparent when I went to see Kedir Tahir Hagos, who leads the implementation of the Ethiopian pharmaceutical sector development strategy. It was difficult to even pin him down for a meeting, because he spends his days shuttling between the Ministry of Industry, the Ministry of Health, the food and drug regulator, and a dozen other entities that must get on board to make this work. In his bare and run-down office, I asked him what his three top priorities were for the coming year. He proceeded to list no fewer than nine items, ranging from helping local manufacturers achieve good practice standards to developing a university major on pharmaceutical regulations to getting a package of incentives for pharmaceutical manufacturing codified into law.[32] For this effort to succeed, the companies, the parliament, and even a new generation of students have roles to play, and getting them to work together in a timely way will be a herculean task.

In addition to the administrative and coordination challenges, the plan will cost substantial amounts of money for a poor country like Ethiopia, whose per capita GDP is only $500—less than half Kenya's and one-sixth Nigeria's, and an astonishing one percent of that in the United States.[33] No one I spoke to could name a single, consolidated cost figure for implementing the pharmaceutical industry development plan, but clearly it will have several types of costs, each one substantial in its own right. To begin with, the Ethiopian government is prepared to pay significantly higher prices for drugs from local suppliers. As in many other countries (including the United States), the government buys a large proportion of the drugs used in the country, and it has decided to pay 25 percent more for locally made drugs.[34] This striking decision echoes both China's and India's privileging of domestic production, even at the expense of near-term public health goals. Along with these direct costs will come significant indirect costs in the form of forgone government revenues. Among the incentives for firms to invest locally are customs duty exemptions, tax deductions, and tax-free loans—meaning that Ethiopian taxpayers will be footing the bill for a large portion of private firms' expansion plans.

In short, creating a domestic pharmaceutical industry in Ethiopia will be both difficult and costly. One way to view these efforts is as an inefficient use of scarce resources—squandering a poor country's national budget, taxpayers' paltry incomes, and the finite time and attention of top-level leaders. Another way, however, is as a bet on the transformational power that a manufacturing industry can have on a nation and a people. It's the belief that competitive advantages are not so much God-given as achieved through hard work and determined action. And it's a recognition that no one can ever accomplish anything hard without at least giving it a try.

If that sounds overly glib, consider that its very glibness serves a purpose. As the late, great economist Albert O. Hirschman observed, a certain amount of overconfidence is necessary for economic development. In a corollary to Adam Smith's "invisible hand" that guides market decisions, Hirschman identified a "Hiding Hand" that obscures difficulties and allows people to embark on projects that are beyond their current ken. He writes, "The Hiding Hand can help accelerate the rate at which 'mankind' engages successfully in problem-solving: it takes up problems *it thinks* it can solve, finds they are really more difficult than expected, but then, being stuck with them, attacks willy-nilly the unsuspected difficulties—and sometimes even succeeds."[35] This is the mental enabler of bootstrapping: if you're overconfident, you're more likely to take on a challenge and more likely to stick with it when it gets hard. Ethiopia is almost certainly overstating its ability to create a domestic pharmaceutical sector; but if it stops to consider all the difficulties right now, it will never try. And if it never tries, it will never succeed. It is no accident that Dr. Arkebe Oqubay, the minister behind many of Ethiopia's industrial development initiatives, prominently cites Hirschman's Hiding Hand in his book.[36]

. . .

There are good arguments for why Ethiopia's pharmaceutical development plan makes sense, but not all are willing to put their money where their mouth is. In 2014, GlaxoSmithKline (GSK), one of the ten largest pharmaceutical companies in the world, announced that it was strongly considering building a drug production facility in Ethiopia.[37] According to staff members at multiple international donors working in Ethiopia, GSK made repeated trips to the country, dangling the possibility of investing in a local production site. Each time, in the words of a person familiar with the visits, the government "bent over backwards" to accommodate GSK's requests and impress the pharma giant. But ultimately, after two years of hoping and enticing, the Ethiopian government was told no. The market was too small, and Ethiopia is too poor. There would be no GSK plant, at least not in the next few years.

In marked contrast, Chinese pharmaceutical firms are seizing the opportunity. I spent a day with some executives of Humanwell Healthcare Group, a Chinese maker of drugs and other medical products. They had followed a timeline similar to GSK's, also beginning to consider a pharmaceutical plant in East Africa in 2014. But unlike GSK, Humanwell was decisive. After two trips, company executives decided to build. The board approved an initial investment of $20 million, with plans to put closer to $100 million into Ethiopia over the long term.[38] In mid-2016, around the time that GSK withdrew its interest, Humanwell broke ground on a new factory in Ethiopia.

When we started the conversation, Tang Yuzhong, Humanwell's general manager for its Ethiopia business, was rather stiff. He cited the company's global growth strategy, Ethiopia's large population, and the Ethiopian government's commitment to health care as rationales for the investment—in other words, standard business speak. This nagged at me, because faced with the exact same factors, GSK decided *not* to invest. But no matter how I phrased the question, Mr. Tang's answers floated on this surface level.

Finally, we left to see the factory site. We drove an hour and a half from Addis Ababa, Ethiopia's capital, into the countryside. An hour into the drive, we started seeing ice in the ditches and gullies alongside the road. It turned out that it had hailed not an hour before. But despite the poor weather, the construction workers were hard at work when we arrived. Two Chinese managers brought us rain boots, and we trudged through the thick mud to inspect the site. I asked the man who handed me my boots how long he had been in Ethiopia. Two days, he replied. I asked him where he was living. He pointed to a row of low makeshift barracks.

This, I think, is the real reason Chinese companies are willing to invest in Africa. Beyond the business speak, there's a personal willingness to live in Africa as it is, and a fearlessness about building its future, come what may. At dinner that night, over steaming, spicy hotpot, Mr. Tang dropped his careful mask at last and reminisced about his childhood growing up in Ürümqi, one of the poorer and more remote parts of China. "The Ürümqi of my childhood was poorer than Ethiopia!" he told me. Another Humanwell manager, also from Ürümqi, concurred. The two of them described a city with almost no modern buildings, where people lived in thatched-roof huts well into the second half of the twentieth century. Not to be left out, the third executive at the dinner cut in: "We had huts like that where I grew up in Hubei, too!"

It might be easy to dismiss this conversation as merely old hands comparing war scars, but a deeper truth is reflected in their banter. There is a profound match between China and Africa in this historical moment. The structural reason Humanwell sees investment in Ethiopia as obvious—whereas GSK, presented with the exact same facts, sees it as untenable—is that investors from developing countries are more natural investors in other developing countries. Humanwell is used to doing business in China, which requires a much more similar way of doing business to Ethiopia than the United Kingdom does. Chinese firms also tend to have a more complementary product mix for African consumers and more labor-intensive operations, which are a better fit for Africa. In economics terms, China and Ethiopia have a similar factor endowment.

Equally important, Chinese firms employ a host of people who are willing to tough it out in environments that few from the developed world are willing to handle for long. These are people who are willing to not see their families for a year, people who are willing to get off a plane and go straight to live in a mud-field, people whose entire livelihoods center on building factories in seemingly inhospitable places. These entrepreneurs and managers possess an irreplaceable set of tacit knowledge about development. This is lived experience—no textbook or donors' conference or development economics program can quite capture its essence— and its relocation to Africa brings a gift beyond investment dollars alone.

But perhaps most important, the Chinese showing up in Africa—whether government officials or migrant entrepreneurs— believe that Africa is in the same position China itself was a few short decades ago. Underneath their gruffness, they think there's no reason Africa won't become rich as well, and soon. A pervasive sense of the personal—where *I* was, what *I* experienced when *my* country developed itself—sets Chinese apart from Westerners attempting to foster development in Africa. There are no pilot projects, no NGOs, no theorizing about paths to development— only the blunt attempt to re-create what China built for itself over the past three decades.

During my first trip to research Chinese investment in Africa, I spent a few days in another muddy field, this one in southern Nigeria. I was standing in what was supposed to be an industrial zone, but I could see little evidence of that. Less than 500 meters past the impressive main gate, the paved road gave out to a dirt trail. There was no power and no water. The Chinese zone managers lived in low, warehouselike buildings scattered near dirt roads, little clearings amid the bush. A mere two years later, this same site would become the Ogun Guangdong Free Trade Zone, which despite recent turmoil still constitutes the largest source of non-oil customs revenue in Nigeria and generates employment for thousands of local people. But on that first visit, I was hard-pressed to imagine it.

The Chinese man who showed me around had no such lack of imagination. He was confident of what Africa can become. "Chinese people of my generation are very clear where Africa is on China's path of development," he told me. "This is exactly like my hometown thirty years ago. If we could do it, then so can this place."

Feeling the Stones

While all things are theoretically possible at all times, history nonetheless presents openings during which change is most probable. This book describes one such moment for Africa. Right now, the confluence of rising labor costs in China, the relocation of Chinese factory owners with valuable life experiences to Africa, and Africa's demographics makes it possible for us to imagine that Africa might very well become the next Factory of the World.

But if Africa's industrialization is predicated on Chinese investment, will it be endangered as China's economy slows? Indeed, from growth rates of nearly 10 percent a year for three decades, Chinese economic growth has dropped to a more modest though still enviable 5–7 percent a year. But there is ample reason to believe that rather than impeding the phenomenon of Chinese investment in Africa, the slowdown will accelerate the relocation of firms abroad. Lower returns on capital domestically will drive Chinese companies to spend their investment dollars offshore. China's aging demographics, irreversible in the short and medium term, mean that excess labor has dried up at home, making its manufacturing operations increasingly likely to move to countries with lower labor costs. And as good opportunities dry up in

China, increasing numbers of Chinese will find opportunities in Africa relatively more attractive. As the site manager of a Chinese heavy equipment installation and maintenance project in Kenya told me, "Back in 2014, when things were still good in China, technicians were demanding all kinds of things to come to Africa. They were cocky! But now [in 2016], there aren't so many jobs in China. They are *guai*, and they are happy with the salaries we offer them here." *Guai* is the term Chinese people use to describe docile children.

A second challenge to the argument laid out in this book is the rapid advance of robotics and automation. If robots take over manufacturing work, there will be no need to reduce labor costs and hence no reason for factories to relocate. While I don't claim to be an expert on this topic, I suspect that many of the most vocal proponents of this theory have never actually been inside a labor-intensive factory, or met the entrepreneurs behind it. It may already be technically possible for robots to take the place of humans; but spend a day inside Mrs. Shen's clothing factory, from chapter 3, and it will be obvious why humans are still indispensable to her business model. Mrs. Shen has to ramp up her entire factory to make a totally different style several times a year, so it makes no sense to put vast amounts of capital toward making any one particular style. Furthermore, her margins are thin—where can she raise the money for such expensive, state-of-the-art machinery? The essential point automation alarmists miss is that technological adoption happens through millions of individual decisions by companies that are constrained by the demands of their value chain, the financing capability of their balance sheets, and their own managerial know-how. Just because they could produce something in a more automated way doesn't mean they will. James Manyika, the coauthor of a recent McKinsey report on automation that concluded much the same thing, says, "This is going to take decades. How automation affects employment will not be decided simply by what is technically feasible, which is what technologists tend to focus on."[1]

Yet one can reasonably point out that the clothing subsector is unique within the manufacturing sector: few factories require so much task flexibility on such rapid timelines. The vast majority of factories crank out much larger batches of much more similar goods and hence are ripe for automation. Yet this objection ignores the fact that most factories are *already* highly automated. Take a stroll in the Formosa denim cloth factory, from chapter 3, and you'll run into a few dozen humans across vast factory spaces. That is to say, unlike what robotics alarmists would have you believe, no clear break exists between our so-called robotics age and what came before: as long as manufacturing has existed, factories have continually introduced new labor-saving technologies. The assembly line, precision tooling machines, automated wire-guided vehicles, computer numerical control systems—all these are major labor-saving technologies that are widespread in manufacturing. One might think that each time such a technology is introduced, manufacturing jobs will disappear, yet that has never been the case. Human ingenuity in inventing new products and human voracity in consuming ever more goods per person have ensured the continued expansion of manufacturing output and manufacturing jobs, even as it takes fewer people to produce each unit of output. And as Asia and Africa—the bulk of the global population—get richer on the backs of these very manufacturing jobs, they will create more consumer demand to continue to fuel the manufacturing sector.

. . .

The opening for Africa to become the next Factory of the World coincides with another shift: as Western countries turn inward, China is increasingly turning outward. In late 2013, Chinese President Xi Jinping announced the Belt and Road strategy, which seeks to rebuild the old Silk Road across Asia, Europe, and Africa into a modern trade superhighway. The initiative is breathtaking in its ambition: to connect more than half the world's population and a third of global GDP. In January 2017, a mere two months after US voters elected Donald Trump on a platform of "America First" and six months after British voters opted to leave the European Union, Xi gave a rousing defense of globalization at the World Economic Forum in Davos, Switzerland. Responding implicitly to Trump's withdrawal of the United States from pursuing major trade deals with Asia and Europe, Xi asserted, "No one would emerge as a winner in a global trade war. Pursuing protectionism is just like locking oneself in a dark room. Wind and rain might be kept outside but so are light and air."[2]

China is the first developing country to assume such a global leadership position in modern history. With that position comes the possibility of reinventing development. The will is clearly there, as are the funds: China took the lead in launching the $100 billion Asian Infrastructure Investment Bank and the $40 billion Silk Road Fund and joined the other BRICS countries (Brazil, Russia, India, and South Africa) to launch the $100 billion New Development Bank. These moves together represent the biggest rebalancing in global development finance since the creation of the International Monetary Fund and the World Bank at Bretton Woods in 1944. In their ambition and scale, these new banks have the potential to match their forebears not only in financing capacity but in global agenda-setting clout.

How should China use this power? As China steps out onto the global stage with grand strategies and lofty new institutions, the lesson from this book is that true development happens elsewhere. It happens in factories and shops, in run-down government offices and on unwieldy pieces of industrial machinery, in the aspirations of men trying to start their own businesses and the spirit of women going to work for the first time. True development is a micro process, not a macro one. For the development institutions of this moment to chart a new path past the failures of their predecessors, they must refashion global development to be more humble, more creative, and more responsive to changing conditions and emerging opportunities. Two generations ago, China pioneered this approach when Deng Xiaoping called for his country to "cross the river by feeling the stones"—advice that recognizes the limits of grand planning and instead privileges learning and flexibility. Rather than re-creating and extending an ossified global development industry, with its theories and its experts, the new institutions backed by developing countries should aim for a different model, one that rejects dogma and reflects their own incremental, idiosyncratic experiences.

In so doing, Africa may very well not only match but outdo the development success of China and other countries that have come before. In Kenya, I sat down with Dr. Richard Leakey, the famed conservationist who discovered Turkana Boy, one of the key fossil links between humans and our hominoid ancestors. The brilliant and rebellious son of the paleoanthropologists Louis and Mary Leakey, Richard has led the sort of adventurous life that even movie stars are drawn to. (Angelina Jolie has asked to make a movie about him.[3]) In addition to his scientific exploits, Richard is active in the political sphere, serving in the past as a government minister and now as the chairman of the Kenya Wildlife Service board of trustees. As such, he reviews the environmental impact of proposed infrastructure projects. Two years ago, the Kenyan government contracted with the China Road and Bridge Corporation to build a standard gauge railway from Mombasa to Nairobi. The proposed route cut right through Nairobi National Park, where endangered elephants, giraffes, and lions roam. The international conservation community immediately denounced the decision. But Richard didn't jump to conclusions. He thought about the issue from multiple perspectives—environmental, economic, and human—and didn't assume that they were necessarily in conflict with one another.

"To think that the vast sizes of these national parks cannot be crossed seems unrealistic," he declared when we sat down in his office. He rejected the notion that conservation requires an unchanging vision of Kenya's national parks. "When conservationists say, 'There will never be a road across the Serengeti—it's too precious,' they're speaking with a full stomach, a pension, a nice house, and recreation!" He challenged himself to look at it from the perspective of someone who didn't have those things. "Why not think about how rail and roads and oil can develop without threating the environment?" His tufts of eyebrow hair quivered as if to emphasize the point. In that spirit, he's been reconceiving the role of the environmentalist as someone who helps create what he terms "clever infrastructure" that meets both animal and human needs.[4]

Richard went to the Chinese engineers in charge of building the train tracks and explored several options. One idea was to move the proposed route to a less-obtrusive part of the park. Another involved tunneling the track underground. (This idea was eventually dismissed out of concern that the vibrations would disrupt the lives of many more animals than the tunnel would help.) The real stroke of brilliance was the idea of raising the tracks—much as highways are elevated in sections of the US interstate system. The trains could pass overhead, and the animals could pass under them.

I asked Richard whether the Chinese construction company was resistant to his suggestions. "They've been very cooperative," he responded. "They were not annoyed, or fighting us." He pointed out that in this case, the Kenyan government was the contracting entity and hence the decision maker. In their roles as contractors and technicians, the Chinese were very willing to explore what would make their client happy. But more generally, he believes that the relationship with China is fruitful for Africa. As he put it, "China is a big part of Africa's solutions, not a cause of our problems." Richard is the sort of iconoclastic thinker and doer who breaks down false dichotomies: between African and

Chinese interests, between humans and animals, between development and nature. He is not afraid to challenge assumptions and brainstorm new approaches to old problems. Ideas like his offer the possibility that Africans will not only develop but invent a better way of doing so.

. . .

Zooming out from both Africa and China, this story means something for the rest of us as well, in the sense that it offers an opportunity to interrogate and clarify what development entails. It is not about grand ideas and dogma but, rather, about incremental change and creativity under trying circumstances. And although Richard Leakey figures prominently in this last example, more than high-level politicians and high-profile leaders, such change takes seemingly ordinary people. It is striking that almost none of the remarkable people in this book define themselves as "development" people. By and large, they are not world leaders, economists, philanthropists, aid workers, or any of the various classes whose primary occupation is to help those in less-fortunate circumstances. Rather, they are entrepreneurs, managers, workers on the line, climbers and dreamers. They are profit-seeking, sometimes generous but often self-interested, sometimes prescient but often myopic in their considerations. They are imperfect, like all the rest of us, and they are the ones in the middle of the rushing river of industrialization right now, feeling the stones. They discover that one is a barrier, and another is a foothold. It is they who come up with ingenious business models, novel uses for a seemingly limited product, innovative ways of configuring organizations, new modes of being in old societies. It looks precarious, sometimes outright dangerous. Progress is uneven and will continue to be so. But it is still the surest way across.

~~rs and John Chambers, "Sovereign Defaults Set to Fall
~~ard & Poor's RatingsDirect, from Laura Alfaro and Ingrid
~~in Sovereign Debt: 'Vulture' Tactics or Market Back-
~~Harvard Business School, 2007).

NOTES

Introduction

1. 2014 share of global manufacturing output figure from Mark Levinson, "U.S. Manufacturing in International Perspective," Congressional Research Service, April 26, 2016, https://fas.org/sgp/crs/misc/R42135.pdf. China's GDP was $358,973.23 in 1990 and grew to $10,866,444.00 in 2015 (World Bank, "GDP [current US$]," http://data.worldbank.org/indicator/NY.GDP.MKTP .CD?end=2015&name_desc=false&start=1990).

2. Per capita GDP figures from the World Bank, "GDP per capita (current US$)," http://data.worldbank.org/indicator/NY.GDP.PCAP .CD?end=2015&name_desc=false&start=1990. In 1990, China's per capita GDP was $316.20, Kenya's $365.60, Lesotho's $340.90, Nigeria's $321.70, and the United States' $23,954.50. Today, although the US economy remains largest in nominal terms, China's is the largest in purchasing power parity (World Bank, "GDP ranking, PPP based," http://data.worldbank.org/data-catalog/GDP-PPP-based-table).

3. "FAW Profile," from FAW's company website. http://www.faw.com /aboutFaw/aboutFaw.jsp?pros=Profile.jsp&phight=580&about=Profile.

4. Center for International Development at Harvard University, "Growth Projections based on 2014 Global Trade Data," *The Atlas of Economic Complexity,* http://atlas.cid.harvard.edu/rankings/growth-predictions-list/.

5. Chinese Ministry of Commerce (MOFCOM) registration list, 2015 data pull.

6. Irene Yuan Sun, Kartik Jayaram, and Omid Kassiri, "Dance of the Lions & Dragons: How Are Africa and China Engaging, and How Will the Partnership Evolve?" McKinsey & Company, June 2017, www.mckinsey.com/africa-china.

7. Chinese government aid to Africa is considerably less than many press reports have suggested, owing to the fact that projects financed by the China Development Bank and the China Exim Bank are often erroneously believed to be official development assistance (the official definition of aid does not include nonconcessional loans and export credits). For a thorough and multifaceted exploration of Chinese aid and economic engagement with Africa, see Deborah

Brautigam, *The Dragon's Gift: The Real Story of China in Africa* (Oxford, UK: Oxford University Press, 2009).

8. Chinua Achebe, *The Education of a British-Protected Child* (New York: Knopf, 2009), 39.

9. Lesotho HIV rate from the CIA World Factbook, 2014 estimate, https://www.cia.gov/library/publications/the-world-factbook/rankorder/2155rank.html.

10. According to the World Bank, "China alone accounted for most of the decline in extreme poverty over the past three decades. Between 1981 and 2011, 753 million people moved above the $1.90-a-day threshold." In 2012, 388.7 million people in sub-Saharan Africa lived in extreme poverty. World Bank, "Poverty: Overview," http://www.worldbank.org/en/topic/poverty/overview.

Chapter 1

1. United Nations Industrial Development Organization (UNIDO), *Industrial Development Report 2009: Breaking In and Moving Up: New Industrial Challenges for the Bottom Billion and the Middle-Income Countries* (New York: United Nations, 2009).

2. Dani Rodrik, "An African Growth Miracle? The Ninth Annual Richard H. Sabot Lecture" (Washington, DC: Center for Global Development, April 2014).

3. Dani Rodrik, "Unconditional Convergence in Manufacturing," *Quarterly Journal of Economics* 128, no. 1 (February 2013).

4. Dani Rodrik, "Goodbye Washington Consensus, Hello Washington Confusion? A Review of the World Bank's *Economic Growth in the 1990s: Learning from a Decade of Reform*," *Journal of Economic Literature* 44 (December 2006): 973–987. The classic formulation of the ten policy instruments generally considered to make up the Washington Consensus comes from John Williamson, who formalized the package in 1989. See John Williamson, ed., *Latin American Adjustment: How Much Has It Happened?* (Washington, DC: Institute for International Economics, 1990).

5. John Williamson, "Did the Washington Consensus Fail?" (Washington, DC: Peterson Institute for International Economics, November 6, 2002), http://www.iie.com/publications/papers/paper.cfm?ResearchID=488.

6. David T. Beers and John Chambers, "Sovereign Defaults Set to Fall Again in 2005," Standard & Poor's RatingsDirect, from Laura Alfaro and Ingrid Vogel, "Creditor Activism in Sovereign Debt: 'Vulture' Tactics or Market Backbone," Case 706057 (Boston: Harvard Business School, 2007).

7. Rodrik, "Goodbye Washington Consensus, Hello Washington Confusion?"

8. Abdelmalek Alaoui, "How African Economics Killed 'The Leapfrog Effect,'" *Forbes*, October 22, 2014, http://www.forbes.com/sites/abdelmalekalaoui /2014/10/22/how-african-economics-killed-the-leapfrog-effect/.

9. Sun Jian, interview by author, Ogun, Nigeria, July 2, 2014.

10. Nobuya Haraguchi and Gorazd Rezonja, "Patterns of Manufacturing Development Revisited," United Nations Industrial Development Organization working paper 22/2009, 2010.

11. Population figures from 1990 are from the World Bank, http://data .worldbank.org/indicator/SP.POP.TOTL. China's share of global manufacturing output in 1990 from "Global Manufacturing: Made in China?" *The Economist*, March 12, 2015, http://www.economist.com/news/leaders/21646204-asias-dominance-manufacturing-will-endure-will-make-development-harder -others-made.

12. John Page, "The East Asian Miracle: Four Lessons for Development Policy," *NBER Macroeconomics Annual 1994,* http://www.nber.org/chapters/c11011.pdf.

13. Eugenio Bregolat, *The Second Chinese Revolution* (Basingstoke, UK: Palgrave Macmillan, 2014).

14. Ibid.

15. "Made in China?" *The Economist*, March 14, 2015, http://www.economist .com/news/leaders/21646204-asias-dominance-manufacturing-will-endure -will-make-development-harder-others-made.

16. World Bank, "Poverty: Overview," http://www.worldbank.org/en /topic/poverty/overview.

17. National Bureau of Statistics, China, GDP data for 1980–1997 in Chinese yuan.

Chapter 2

1. See Rachel Bright, *Chinese Labour in South Africa, 1902–10: Race, Violence, and Global Spectacle* (Basingstoke, UK: Palgrave Macmillan, 2013). For more on the several centuries of Chinese contact with and migration to Africa, see Li Anshan, *A History of Chinese Overseas in Africa* (Beijing: Chinese Overseas Publishing House, 2000).

2. Steve Onyeiwu, "The Modern Textile Industry in Nigeria," *Textile History* 28, no. 2 (1997): 234–249.

3. Salihu Maiwada and Ellisha Renne, "The Kaduna Textile Industry," *Textile History* 44, no. 2 (2013): 171–196.

4. Sola Akinrinade and Olukoya Ogen, "Globalization and De-Industrialization: South-South Neo-Liberalism and the Collapse of the Nigerian Textile Industry," *The Global South* 2, no. 2 (2008): 159–170.

5. Ibid.

6. Ibid.

7. Maiwada and Renne, "The Kaduna Textile Industry."

8. Ibid.

9. Akinrinade and Ogen, "Globalization and De-Industrialization."

10. Ibid.

11. Ibid.

12. Ibid.

13. Onyeiwu, "The Modern Textile Industry in Nigeria."

14. L. N. Chete, J. O. Adeoti, F. M. Adeyinka, and O. Ogundele, "Industrial Development and Growth in Nigeria: Lessons and Challenges," Brookings Africa Growth Initiative Working Paper No. 8., The Brookings Institution, 2016.

15. BigBen Chukwuma Ogbonna, "Structural Adjustment Program (SAP) in Nigeria: An Empirical Assessment," *Journal of Banking* 6, no. 1 (June 2012): 19–40.

16. World Bank Study cited in Onyeiwu, "The Modern Textile Industry in Nigeria."

17. Onyeiwu, "The Modern Textile Industry in Nigeria."

18. Maiwada and Renne, "The Kaduna Textile Industry," 183.

19. Chete, Adeoti, Adeyinka, and Ogundele, "Industrial Development and Growth in Nigeria," 16.

20. BBC News, "Nigeria: 'Oil-Gas Sector Mismanagement Costs Billions,'" October 25, 2012, http://www.bbc.com/news/world-africa-20081268.

21. Lynn Mytelka and Dieter Ernst, "Catching Up, Keeping Up and Getting Ahead: The Korean Model Under Pressure," in Dieter Ernst, Tom Ganiatsos, and Lynn Mytelka, eds, *Technological Capabilities and Export Success in Asia* (London and New York: Routledge, 1998), 96.

22. Jesus Felipe, *Inclusive Growth, Full Employment, and Structural Change: Implications and Policies for Developing Asia*, (Mandaluyong, Philippines: Asian Development Bank, 2012), 86.

23. Ibid., 90.

24. Maiwada and Renne, "The Kaduna Textile Industry."

25. Onyi Sunday, "Africa's Fading Textile Hub," *Guardian* (Nigeria), September 4, 2015, http://www.ngrguardiannews.com/2015/09/africas-fading-textile-hub/.

26. Akinrinade and Ogen, "Globalization and De-Industrialization," 167.

27. Gaaitzen de Vries, Marcel Timmer, and Klaas de Vries, "Structural Transformation in Africa: Static Gains, Dynamic Losses," *Journal of Development Studies* 51, no. 6 (2015): 674–688.

28. Federal Reserve Bank of Chicago, Detroit Branch, "Ballard Discusses Michigan's Economy," December 12, 2012, http://michiganeconomy.chicagofedblogs.org/?p=52. According to these calculations, manufacturing as a percent of gross product in Michigan was nearly 50 percent in 1963 and approximately 15 percent in 2011.

29. "Sector Report: Manufacturing in Africa," Amstelveen, Netherlands: KPMG, 2014.

30. "Nigeria Gets US$1.5 Billion Steel Rolling Plant," *Star Africa*, April 18, 2013.

31. Irene Yuan Sun, Kartik Jayaram, and Omid Kassiri, "Dance of the Lions & Dragons: How Are Africa and China Engaging, and How Will the Partnership Evolve?" McKinsey & Company, June 2017, www.mckinsey.com/africa-china.

32. Yang Wenyi, interview by author, Calabar, Nigeria, July 11, 2014.

33. Juliet Eilpirin and Katie Zezima, "Obama Announces More Investment in Africa by U.S. Firms During Leaders' Summit," *Washington Post*, August 5, 2014, https://www.washingtonpost.com/politics/obama-announces-more-investment-in-africa-by-us-firms/2014/08/05/bb3a9e98-1cd5-11e4-82f9-2cd6fa8da5c4_story.html.

34. Stephen Gordon, "A Little Context on the Decline of Manufacturing Employment in Canada," *Maclean's*, February 12, 2013, http://www.macleans.ca/economy/business/some-context-for-the-decline-in-canadian-manufacturing-employment/, based on data from the St. Louis Federal Reserve FRED database.

35. Dani Rodrik, "On Premature Deindustrialization," Dani Rodrik's weblog, October 11, 2013, http://rodrik.typepad.com/dani_rodriks_weblog/2013/10/on-premature-deindustrialization.html.

36. Robert Lawrence, interview by author, Cambridge, MA, October 7, 2015.

37. Alexander Gerschenkron, *Economic Backwardness in Historical Perspective* (Cambridge, MA: Harvard University Press, 1962).

38. Erich Weede, "Economic Freedom and the Advantages of Backwardness," (Washington, DC: Cato Institute, January 31, 2007), http://www.cato.org/publications/economic-development-bulletin/economic-freedom-advantages-backwardness.

39. "Nigeria Gets US$1.5 Billion Steel Rolling Plant," *Star Africa*.

Notes

Chapter 3

1. Mrs. Shen, interview by author, Maseru, Lesotho, January 19, 2016.

2. Christopher Maloney, "All Dressed Up with No Place to Go: Lesotho's Rollercoaster Experience with Apparel," Harvard Kennedy School SYPA, Cambridge, MA, March 27, 2006.

3. The African Growth and Opportunity Act (AGOA) provides tariff-free access to the US market for qualifying sub-Saharan African countries. It was originally passed in 2000 for eight years. Leading up to 2008, many firms decided to leave Lesotho owing to the uncertainty about AGOA. The United States ultimately extended the act until 2015; in 2015, it was extended again to 2025. Sources: agoa.info, "About AGOA," http://agoa.info/about-agoa.html; interviews by the author in Maseru, Lesotho.

4. Lawrence Edwards and Robert Z. Lawrence, "AGOA Rules: The Intended and Unintended Consequences of Special Fabric Provisions," NBER Working Paper Series 16623, National Bureau of Economic Research, Cambridge, MA, 2010.

5. In 2001, 1,100 of 32,233 workers in Lesotho's apparel sector were foreigners. "Big Textile Investment Push into Lesotho," agoa.info, April 28, 2003, http://agoa.info/news/article/3236-big-textile-investment-push-into-lesotho.html.

6. By using this example, I do not intend to imply that I think Taiwan is or should be the same entity as mainland China. The Formosa mill is the only capital-intensive factory in Lesotho, which makes for a fascinating comparison with labor-intensive clothing factories such as Mrs. Shen's. A further rationale for including a Taiwanese firm in this book about Chinese manufacturing investment in Africa is that anecdotally, many Taiwanese owners are now selling to Chinese owners when they retire.

7. As of May 17, 2016, Nien Hsing's stock was trading at NT 23.65 with 400 million shares outstanding, and the exchange rate was NT 32.59 to US$1. Reuters, http://www.reuters.com/finance/stocks/overview?symbol=1451.TW.

8. Ricky Chang, interview by author, Maseru, Lesotho, January 19, 2016.

9. Formosa denim mill investment size from Lesotho Textile Exporters Association, http://www.lesothotextiles.com/Pages/Lesotho-Textile-Industry.asp?lID=2.

10. John Zhang, interview by author, Calabar, Nigeria, July 11, 2014.

11. "Nigeria gets US$1.5 Billion Steel Rolling Plant," *Star Africa*, April 18, 2003.

12. Mark Bennett, interview by author, Maseru, Lesotho, January 18, 2016.

13. Lesotho's 2015 GDP was US$2.278 billion, according to the World Bank (http://data.worldbank.org/country/lesotho). In 2015, New York's gross metropolitan product was estimated at $1.61 trillion, or $4.41 billion per day ("U.S. Metro

Economies GMP and Employment Report: 2015–2017," The United States Conference of Mayors, January 20, 2016, https://www.usmayors.org/2016/01/20/u-s-metro-economies-gmp-and-employment-report-2015-2017/.

14. World Bank, http://data.worldbank.org/country/nigeria.

15. Jennifer Chen, interview by author, Maseru, Lesotho, January 20, 2016.

16. World Economic Forum, http://reports.weforum.org/global-competitiveness-report-2014-2015/rankings/; World Economic Forum, http://www.doingbusiness.org/rankings.

Chapter 4

1. Alan Lin, interview by author, Maseru, Lesotho, January 20, 2016.

2. Marina Bizabani, interview by author, Maseru, Lesotho, January 21, 2016.

3. Sun Jian, interview by author, Ogun, Nigeria, July 2, 2014.

4. Nigerian businessman (name redacted because he has business dealings with Chinese firms), interview by author, Lagos, Nigeria, July 26, 2013.

5. "Corruption Perceptions Index 2015," Transparency International, https://www.transparency.org/cpi2015/#results-table.

6. I have chosen to withhold the name of this Chinese businessman because of the nature of the activities described. The interview took place in Lagos, Nigeria, in August 2013. I previously published an account of these events in the Nigerian *Guardian*, September 21, 2013.

7. Chinedu Bosah, interview by author, Lagos, Nigeria, August 14, 2013.

8. I previously published an account of this investigation in the Nigerian *Guardian*, October 19, 2013.

9. Rosemary McGee and John Gaventa, "Synthesis Report: Review of Impact and Effectiveness of Transparency and Accountability Initiatives," Transparency Accountability Initiative, 2010, http://www.transparency-initiative.org/wp-content/uploads/2017/03/synthesis_report_final1.pdf, 5.

10. Ibid, 6.

11. Richard A. Greenwald, *The Triangle Fire, the Protocols of Peace, and Industrial Democracy in Progressive Era New York* (Philadelphia: Temple University Press, 2005).

12. Mark Aldrich, *Safety First: Technology, Labor, and Business in the Building of American Work Safety, 1870–1939* (Baltimore: Johns Hopkins University Press, 1997). Mark Aldrich, "History of Workplace Safety in the United States, 1880–1970," Economic History Association, http://eh.net/encyclopedia/history-of-workplace-safety-in-the-united-states-1880-1970/.

13. Author interview with Wu Mingsi, Maseru, Lesotho, January 19, 2016.

Notes

Chapter 5

1. Ahmed Ibrahim, interview by author, Ogun, Nigeria, July 1, 2014.

2. Yan Hairong and Barry Sautman, "Chasing Ghosts: Rumours and Representations of the Export of Chinese Convict Labour to Developing Countries," *China Quarterly* 210 (June 2012): 398–418.

3. Irene Yuan Sun, Kartik Jayaram, and Omid Kassiri, "Dance of the Lions & Dragons: How Are Africa and China Engaging, and How Will the Partnership Evolve?" McKinsey & Company, June 2017, www.mckinsey.com /africa-china.

4. "Business Perception Index Kenya 2014," Sino-Africa Centre of Excellence Foundation, 2014.

5. "The Future of Factory Asia: A Tightening Grip," *The Economist*, March 12, 2015, http://www.economist.com/news/briefing/21646180-rising -chinese-wages-will-only-strengthen-asias-hold-manufacturing-tightening-grip.

6. Justin Yifu Lin, "China's Rise and Structural Transformation in Africa: Ideas and Opportunities," in Célestin Monga and Justin Yifu Lin, eds., *The Oxford Handbook of Africa and Economics, Volume 2: Policies and Practices* (Oxford, UK: Oxford University Press, 2015).

7. "The Shifting Economics of Global Manufacturing," Boston Consulting Group, Boston, MA, August 2014.

8. Mr. Wu, interview by author, Calabar, Nigeria, July 11, 2014.

9. Justin Yifu Lin, "From Flying Geese to Leading Dragons: New Opportunities and Strategies for Structural Transformation in Developing Countries," World Bank, Washington, DC, June 2011, 4. J. Esteban, J. Stiglitz, and Justin Yifu Lin, eds., *The Industrial Policy Revolution II: Africa in the Twenty-first Century* (Basingstoke, UK: Palgrave Macmillan, 2013).

10. Enrico Moretti, *The New Geography of Jobs* (Boston: Mariner, 2013), 21.

11. "Leveraging Africa's Demographic Dividend," *African Business Magazine*, January 14, 2015, http://africanbusinessmagazine.com/uncategorised /leveraging-africas-demographic-dividend/.

12. United Nations Population Division, "World Population Prospects: The 2015 Revision."

13. Ibid.

14. International Labour Organization, "Where Is the Unemployment Rate the Highest in 2014?" http://www.ilo.org/global/about-the-ilo/multimedia /maps-and-charts/WCMS_233936/lang--en/index.htm.

15. Nigeria National Bureau of Statistics (Nigeria), "Unemployment/ Under-employment Watch Q1 2016," May 2016.

16. Ibid.

Notes

17. International Labour Organization, "Where Is the Unemployment Rate the Highest in 2014?"

18. World Bank, "Youth and Unemployment in Africa: The Potential, the Problem, the Promise" (Washington, DC: The World Bank, 2009).

19. Enrico Moretti, *New Geography of Jobs.*

20. Ibid.

21. Kevin Watkins, Justin W. van Fleet, and Lauren Greubel, "Africa Learning Barometer," Brookings Institute, http://www.brookings.edu /research/interactives/africa-learning-barometer.

22. African Development Bank, "Enhancing Capacity for Youth Employment in Africa: Some Emerging Lessons," *Africa Capacity Development Brief* 2, no. 2, December 2011, http://www.afdb.org/fileadmin/uploads/afdb /Documents/Publications/Africa%20Capacity%20Dev%20Brief_Africa%20 Capacity%20Dev%20Brief.pdf.

23. Ibid.

24. Mr. Wang, interview by author, Ogun, Nigeria, July 1, 2014.

25. Chinese manager [name redacted], interview by author, Ogun, Nigeria, June 30, 2014.

26. Lebanese owner-manager [name redacted], interview by author, Ogun, Nigeria, June 30, 2014.

27. Managing director [name redacted], interview by author, Nairobi, Kenya, July 6, 2015.

28. Howard W. French, *China's Second Continent* (New York: Knopf, 2014), 15.

29. Chinese expatriate worker, interview by author, Lagos, Nigeria, July 30, 2016.

30. Incident at Huaiyang Restaurant, Addis Ababa, Ethiopia, July 19, 2016.

31. John Foster, "An Essay on the Evils of Popular Ignorance" (London, 1821), 180–185, quoted in E. P. Thompson, "Time, Work-Discipline, and Industrial Capitalism," *Past & Present* 38 (December 1967), 56–97.

32. Ibid., 73.

33. Ibid.

34. Alexander Gerschenkron, *Economic Backwardness in Historical Perspective*, (Cambridge, MA: Belknap, 1966), 9.

35. *Wall Street Journal*, July 3, 1991, A4.

36. Gerschenkron, *Economic Backwardness*, 9.

37. Leslie T. Chang, *Factory Girls: From Village to City in a Changing China* (New York: Spiegel & Grau, 2008), 74.

38. E. P. Thompson, "Time, Work-Discipline, and Industrial Capitalism," 80.

39. Kelly Pike, interview by the author on Skype, March 10, 2016.

Notes

Chapter 6

1. Stephen Sigei, interview by author, Nairobi, Kenya, July 10, 2016.

2. Larry Hanauer and Lyle J. Morris, *Chinese Engagement in Africa: Drivers, Reactions, and Implications for U.S. Policy*, (Santa Monica, CA: RAND Corporation, 2014), 30–31.

3. Dinah Jerotich Mwinzi, remarks at the Africa Tech Challenge 2016 Opening Ceremony, Nairobi, Kenya, July 12, 2016.

4. Stephen Sigei, interview by author, Nairobi, Kenya, July 10, 2016.

5. Additional locally owned firms are entering the clothing industry, most notably Seshoeshoe, purportedly an approximately 50-person firm producing traditional clothing. However, I was not able to confirm its status as a going concern in person.

6. Bureau of Labor Statistics, "Entrepreneurship and the U.S. Economy," http://www.bls.gov/bdm/entrepreneurship/entrepreneurship.htm.

7. Chris Mohapi, interview by author, Maseru, Lesotho, January 22, 2016.

8. Jennifer Chen, interview by author, Maseru, Lesotho, January 20, 2016.

9. Site visit to Tlotliso factory, Lesotho, January 21, 2016.

10. Thabiso Mothabeng, interview by author, Maseru, Lesotho, January 19, 2016.

11. Luqy Adams, interview by author, Maseru, Lesotho, January 21, 2016.

12. Shegaw Aderaw, Alemayehu Eshete, and Bizualew Mekonnen, interview by author, outside Addis Ababa, Ethiopia, July 21, 2016.

13. Zaf Gebretsadik Tsadik, interview by author, Addis Ababa, Ethiopia, July 25, 2016.

14. Ibid.

15. Salman Rushdie, *Imaginary Homelands* (London: Penguin, 1992), 11.

16. Zi Ran, interviews by author, Nairobi, Kenya, July 9 and November 17, 2016.

17. Xiao Nie and Sang Bu, "呆不下去的非洲, 回不去的中国," 波布非洲 (on WeChat), October 7, 2015.

18. Author's translation. In the original Chinese: "心安之处, 是故乡。...人, 不管什么时候, 都不应该放弃自己的梦想。"

19. Rushdie, *Imaginary Homelands*, 15.

20. Ibid., 15–16.

Chapter 7

1. "Clinton Warns Against 'New Colonialism' in Africa," Reuters World News, June 11, 2011, http://www.reuters.com/article/us-clinton-africa-idUSTRE75A0RI20110611. Kathleen Caulderwood, "China Is Africa's New

Colonial Overlord, Says Famed Primate Researcher Jane Goodall," *International Business Times*, February 18, 2014, http://www.ibtimes.com/china-africas-new -colonial-overlord-says-famed-primate-researcher-jane-goodall-1556312.

2. Boaz Munga and Eldah Onsomu, "State of Youth Unemployment in Kenya," Brookings Institute Africa in Focus, August 21, 2014, http://www .brookings.edu/blogs/africa-in-focus/posts/2014/08/21-state-of-youth -unemployment-kenya-munga.

3. Charles F. Sabel, "Bootstrapping Development: Rethinking the Role of Public Intervention in Promoting Growth" (paper presented at *The Protestant Ethic and the Spirit of Capitalism* Conference, Cornell University, Ithaca, New York; November 14, 2005 version), 7.

4. Transparency International, 2010/2011 Global Corruption Barometer (GCB) Data Set, Question: "% of people that have paid a bribe to each of 9 institutions."

5. Rowena Mason and Richard Blackden, "Shell to Pay $48m Nigerian Bribe Fine," *Telegraph*, November 4, 2010. U.S. Securities and Exchange Commission, "SEC Charges Seven Oil Services and Freight Forwarding Companies for Widespread Bribery of Customs Officials," November 4, 2010, https://www .sec.gov/news/press/2010/2010-214.htm. Propublica, "The World Wide Web of Siemens's Corruption," https://www.propublica.org/special/the-world-wide -web-of-siemenss-corruption.

6. See Douglas Zhihua Zeng, "Global Experiences with Special Economic Zones: Focus on China and Africa," Investing in Africa Forum, Addis Ababa, Ethiopia, February 2015, http://documents.worldbank.org/curated /en/810281468186872492/Global-experiences-with-special-economic-zones -focus-on-China-and-Africa.

7. Tim Maughan, "The Changing Face of Shenzhen, the World's Gadget Factory," *Vice*, August 19, 2015, http://motherboard.vice.com/read/beyond -foxconn-inside-shenzhen-the-worlds-gadget-factory.

8. Sheriff Balogun, "Ogun to Reposition Quandong Free Trade Zone," *This Day Live*, June 18, 2012.

9. "Customs Generates N2 bn in Four Months in Ogun," *NaijaMotherland*, June 8, 2015, http://www.nigeriannewspapers.today/customs-generates -n2-bn-in-four-months-in-ogun/. Jason Han and John Xue, interview by author, Beijing, China, June 25, 2015.

10. Stephen Knack and Nicholas Eubank, "Aid and Trust in Country Systems," World Bank, Washington, DC, 2009, https://openknowledge.worldbank.org /handle/10986/4197.

11. Ibid.

12. John Xue, interview by author by phone, February 21, 2016.

13. Ibid.

14. M-Pesa has 19 million users in Kenya. Lilian Ochieng, "M-Pesa Reports 27 pc Jump in Global Users to 25 Million," *Daily Nation*, April 27, 2016, http://www.nation.co.ke/business/M-Pesa-reports-27-pc-jump-in-global-users-to-25-million/996-3178018-5ykpjpz/index.html. Kenya's population in 2015 was 45.9 million, of which 41.6% were children aged 0–14. The World Factbook Kenya, Central Intelligence Agency, https://www.cia.gov/library/publications/the-world-factbook/geos/ke.html.

15. Claudia McKay and Rafe Mazer, "10 Myths About M-PESA: 2014 Update," CGAP, October 1, 2014, http://www.cgap.org/blog/10-myths-about-m-pesa-2014-update; and Tonny K. Omwansa and Nicholas P. Sullivan, *Money, Real Quick: The Story of M-PESA* (London: Guardian Books, 2012).

16. Ibid. Kenya population of 46 million from the World Bank (2015), http://data.worldbank.org/country/kenya. World population of 7.3 billion from the US Census Bureau, https://www.census.gov/popclock/world.

17. https://bizextras.wordpress.com/2011/05/23/so-who-invented-m-pesa/.

18. Omwansa and Sullivan, *Money, Real Quick*.

19. Ibid.

20. Michael Joseph, interview by author, Cambridge, MA, April 14, 2016.

21. Bitange Ndemo, interview by author, Nairobi, Kenya, July 11, 2016.

22. Omwansa and Sullivan, *Money, Real Quick*.

23. Ibid.

24. Njuguna Ndung'u, interview by author, Nairobi, Kenya, July 8, 2016.

25. Mukhisa Kituyi, "Kenya's Mobile Money Innovation Draws World Attention," *Daily Nation*, May 21, 2011, http://www.nation.co.ke/oped/Opinion/Kenyas+mobile+money+innovation+draws+world+attention+/-/440808/1166842/-/kctp0xz/-/index.html.

26. Tony Saich, *Governance and Politics of China* (3rd edition) (Basingstoke, UK: Palgrave Macmillan, 2010), 5, 7.

27. Ibid., 4.

28. Peter J. Katzenstein, *Small States in World Markets: Industrial Policy in Europe* (Ithaca, NY: Cornell University Press, 1985), 79.

29. GDP numbers from 1950. Angus Maddison, *Contours of the World Economy, 1–2030 AD* (Oxford, UK: Oxford University Press, 2007).

30. Oliver Rathkolb, a prominent scholar of Austria, writes, "Austrian economic policy in the first years after 1945 largely indirectly continued the 'Aryanization' policy of the Nazi regime in its structural effects." Some specific policy examples: Austria declined to restore most Jewish-owned businesses seized during WWII to their rightful owners, and even defined citizenship in a way that made it difficult for Jewish exiles to return after the war. Oliver Rathkolb, translated from the German by Otmar Binder, Eleanor Breuning, Ian

Notes

Fraser, and David Sinclair-Jones, *The Paradoxical Republic: Austria, 1945–2005* (Berghahn Books, German edition 2005, English edition 2010), 61–62.

31. Peter J. Katzenstein, *Corporatism and Change: Austria, Switzerland, and the Politics of Industry* (Ithaca, NY: Cornell University Press, 1987), 58.

32. Africa Tech Challenge 2016 opening ceremony, Nairobi, Kenya, July 12, 2016.

33. Qian Rong, interview by author, Nairobi, Kenya, July 12, 2016.

Chapter 8

1. amfAR, The Foundation for AIDS Research, "Statistics: Worldwide," http://www.amfar.org/worldwide-aids-stats/.

2. World Health Organization, "TB/HIV facts 2012–2013," http://www.who.int/hiv/topics/tb/tbhiv_facts_2013/en/. Johns Hopkins Malaria Research Institute, "About Malaria," http://malaria.jhsph.edu/about-malaria/.

3. UN Inter-agency Group for Child Mortality Estimation, "Levels & Trends in Child Mortality: Report 2014," http://www.unicef.org/media/files/Levels_and_Trends_in_Child_Mortality_2014.pdf. World Health Organization, "Maternal Mortality (Fact Sheet, Updated November 2016)," http://www.who.int/mediacentre/factsheets/fs348/en/.

4. World Health Organization, "Child and Adolescent Health and Nutrition," http://www.afro.who.int/en/clusters-a-programmes/frh/child-and-adolescent-health/programme-components/child-health.html.

5. The Global Fund, http://www.theglobalfund.org/en/financials/. GAVI, "Annual Contributions and Proceeds to GAVI 30 June 2016," downloadable at http://www.gavi.org/funding/donor-contributions-pledges/annual-contributions-and-proceeds/.

6. Avert, "Funding for HIV and AIDS," http://www.avert.org/funding-hiv-and-aids.htm.

7. Price of antiretroviral drugs in 1987 from "AZT's Inhuman Cost," *New York Times*, August 28, 1989, http://www.nytimes.com/1989/08/28/opinion/azt-s-inhuman-cost.html. Recent prices from "CHAI, UNITAID, and DFID Announce Lower Prices for HIV/AIDS Medicines in Developing Countries," UNITAID, May 17, 2011, http://www.unitaid.eu/en/resources/331-clinton-health-access-initiative-unitaid-and-dfid-announce-lower-prices-for-hivaids-medicines-in-developing-countries.

8. UNAIDS, "UNAIDS Announces That the Goal of 15 Million People on Life-saving HIV Treatment by 2015 Has Been Met Nine Months Ahead of Schedule," http://www.unaids.org/en/resources/presscentre/pressreleaseandstatementarchive/2015/july/20150714_PR_MDG6report.

9. Global Fund, "Tuberculosis," https://www.theglobalfund.org/en/tuberculosis/.

10. Mark Grabowsky and Katherine Rockwell, "With One Year to Go, What the Data Say About MDG4 Progress and Gaps," Office of the UN Secretary-General's Special Envoy for Health in Agenda 2030 and for Malaria, http://www.mdghealthenvoy.org/with-one-year-to-go-what-the-data-say-about-mdg4-progress-and-gaps/. World Bank, "Improve Maternal Health by 2015," http://www5.worldbank.org/mdgs/maternal_health.html.

11. John Kerry, "Remarks at the President's Emergency Plan for AIDS Relief (PEPFAR) 10th Anniversary Celebration," https://2009-2017.state.gov/secretary/remarks/2013/06/210770.htm.

12. Germany has 920 drug manufacturers, to be exact. Germany Trade & Invest, "Pharmaceutical Industry," http://www.gtai.de/GTAI/Navigation/EN/Invest/Industries/Life-sciences/pharmaceuticals.html.

13. Federal Democratic Republic of Ethiopia, Ministry of Health and Ministry of Industry, "National Strategy and Plan of Action for Pharmaceutical Manufacturing Development in Ethiopia (2015–2025)," abridged version, July 2015.

14. Samuel Wangwe, Paula Tibandebage, Edwin Mhede, Caroline Israel, Phares Mujinja, and Maureen Mackintosh, "Reversing Pharmaceutical Manufacturing Decline in Tanzania: Policy Options and Constraints," *Policy Research for Development* 43 (July 2014), http://www.repoa.or.tz/documents/REPOA_BRIEF_43.pdf.

15. Dan Munro, "Ebola: While Big Pharma Slept," *Forbes*, September 14, 2014, http://www.forbes.com/sites/danmunro/2014/09/14/ebola-while-big-pharma-slept/#a8293ee6627a; and Mirjam Gehrke, "Pharmaceutical Industry Neglects Developing Countries," *Deutsche Welle*, October 26, 2012, http://p.dw.com/p/16WgN.

16. Doctors Without Borders, "No Time to Quit: HIV/AIDS Treatment Gap Widening in Africa," May 2010, http://www.doctorswithoutborders.org/sites/usa/files/MSF-No-Time-to-Quit-HIV-AIDS.pdf.

17. Daniel Berman, interview by author on Skype, July 22, 2016.

18. Yanzhong Huang, "Chinese Pharma: A Global Health Game Changer?" Council on Foreign Relations, New York, March 31, 2015, http://www.cfr.org/china/chinese-pharma-global-health-game-changer/p36365.

19. Viral Shah, "Evolution of Pharmaceutical Industry: A Global Indian & Gujarat Perspective," *Journal of Pharmaceutical Science and Bioscientific Research* 2, no. 5, Sept–Oct 2012, 219–229, http://www.jpsbr.org/index_htm_files/5_JPSBR_12_RV109.pdf.

20. Von Richard Gerster, "The success story of the Indian pharmaceutical industry," *Medicus Mundi Schweiz*, MMS Bulletin #84, April 2002, http://www .medicusmundi.ch/de/bulletin/mms-bulletin/zugang-zu-medikamenten/zur -rolle-der-pharmaindustrie/the-success-story-of-the-indian-pharmaceutical -industry.

21. Shelly Weiss and Dave Forrester, "China's Pharmaceutical Industry," *China Business Review* 31, no. 6 (Nov/Dec 2004), 16–17. "Building Up Com- petitiveness and Sustainability: A Global Perspective on China's Pharmaceutical Industry," *China Chemical Reporter*, January 6, 2010, 17–18.

22. Shufang Huang, "How Can Innovation Create the Future in a Catching-up Economy?" *Journal of Knowledge-Based Innovation in China* 4, no. 2 (2012): 118–131.

23. Pradeep S. Mehta, "TRIPS and Pharmaceuticals: Implications for India," *Schweizerisches Jahrbuch für Entwicklungspolitik* 17 (1998): 97–106.

24. John LaMattina, "India's Solution to Drug Costs: Ignore Patents and Control Prices—Except for Home Grown Drugs," *Forbes*, April 8, 2013, http:// www.forbes.com/sites/johnlamattina/2013/04/08/indias-solution-to-drug -costs-ignore-patents-and-control-prices-except-for-home-grown-drugs /#6146a09c5c46. Alex Philippidis, "Rougher Passage to India's Drug Market," *Genetic Engineering & Biotechnology News*, February 21, 2014, http://www .genengnews.com/insight-and-intelligence/rougher-passage-to-india-s-drug -market/77900044/.

25. Correspondence with a senior staff member (who asked to remain anonymous owing to ongoing projects with the Indian government) of a major Geneva-based global health organization, September 5, 2016.

26. South African Government News Agency, "Government Establishes Pharmaceutical Company," February 11, 2016, http://www.sanews.gov.za/south -africa/government-establishes-pharmaceutical-company. Ina Skosana, "New State-Run Pharmaceutical Company to Produce ARVs by 2019," Bhekisisa Centre for Health Journalism, http://bhekisisa.org/article/2016-02-17-new -state-run-pharmaceutical-company-to-produce-arvs-by-2019.

27. United Nations Industrial Development Organization, "Kenya Phar- maceutical Sector Development Strategy," 2012. Author Skype interview with Daniel Berman, July 22, 2016.

28. Haddis Tadesse, interview by author, Addis Ababa, Ethiopia, July 19, 2016.

29. Government of Ethiopia and World Health Organization, "Launch of Ethiopian National Strategy and Plan of Action for Pharmaceutical Manufactur- ing Development and Improving Access," July 14, 2015.

30. Federal Democratic Republic of Ethiopia Ministry of Health and Ministry of Industry, "National Strategy and Plan of Action for Pharmaceutical Manufacturing Development in Ethiopia (2015–2025)," abridged version, July 2015.

31. Government of Ethiopia and World Health Organization, "Launch of Ethiopian National Strategy," 6.

32. Kedir Tahir Hagos, interview by author, Addis Ababa, Ethiopia, July 25, 2016.

33. According to the World Bank, Ethiopia had a 2015 per capita GDP of $619, Kenya of $1,377, Nigeria of $2,640, and the United States of $55,837. The World Bank, "GDP per capita (current US$)," http://data.worldbank.org /indicator/NY.GDP.PCAP.CD.

34. Federal Democratic Republic of Ethiopia Ministry of Health and Ministry of Industry, "National Strategy and Plan of Action."

35. Albert O. Hirschman, *Development Projects Observed* (Washington, DC: Brookings Institution Press, 2015), 12–13.

36. Arkebe Oqubay, *Made in Africa: Industrial Policy in Ethiopia* (Oxford, UK: Oxford University Press, 2015).

37. GlaxoSmithKline ranked #8 on *Forbes*'s 2015 list of the largest pharmaceutical companies (Liyan Chen, "2015 Global 2000: The World's Largest Drug and Biotech Companies," *Forbes*, June 4, 2015, http://www.forbes.com/sites /liyanchen/2015/06/04/2015-global-2000-the-worlds-largest-drug-and -biotech-companies/#398f29da5768. News reports of GSK's plans to invest in Ethiopia include Eskedar Kifle, "GSK Selects Ethiopia to Manufacture ARV, Antibiotics," *Capital Ethiopia*, April 15, 2014, http://capitalethiopia.com/2014 /04/15/gsk-selects-ethiopia-to-manufacture-arv-antibiotics/#.WPETz1KZOcY and *All Africa*, "Africa: GlaxoSmithKline Considers Ethiopia as a Strategic Country for Investment in Africa," February 12, 2015, http://allafrica.com /stories/201502121731.html. This was also confirmed by my interviews in the Ethiopia offices of the Gates Foundation and the Tony Blair Africa Governance Initiative.

38. Tang Yuzhong, interview by author, July 23, 2016, and "Humanwell Pharmaceutical Ethiopia PLC Project Description" (obtained from company representatives July 23, 2016).

Epilogue

1. Steve Lohr, "Robots Will Take Jobs, but Not as Fast as Some Fear, New Report Says," *New York Times*, January 12, 2017, https://www.nytimes.com /2017/01/12/technology/robots-will-take-jobs-but-not-as-fast-as-some-fear -new-report-says.html?_r=0. See also McKinsey Global Institute, "Harnessing

Notes

Automation for a Future that Works," http://www.mckinsey.com/global
-themes/digital-disruption/harnessing-automation-for-a-future-that-works.

2. Matt Clinch, "China President Xi Jinping: 'No One Will Emerge as a
Winner in a Trade War,'" CNBC, January 17, 2017, http://www.cnbc.com
/2017/01/17/chinas-president-xi-jinping-takes-to-the-stage-at-world-economic
-forum-in-davos.html.

3. Graham Boynton, "Richard Leakey: What Does Angelina Jolie See in
This Man?" *Telegraph*, September 23, 2014, http://www.telegraph.co.uk/culture
/film/film-news/11114617/Richard-Leakey-What-does-Angelina-Jolie-see-in
-this-man.html.

4. Richard Leakey, interview by author, Nairobi, Kenya, July 6, 2016.

INDEX

Index

Index

ACKNOWLEDGMENTS

I am deeply grateful to the people whom I've had the privilege of writing about in this book. Thank you for letting me into your lives—that cup of tea you poured, that glimpse inside your factory, that conversation that probably lasted a bit longer than you had expected. By leading your extraordinary lives, you are reshaping Africa and China. I have been reshaped as well, by watching you, talking to you, and in some small way understanding you. Thank you for this honor.

Although I had some of the most interesting material in the world to work with, this book would not have been possible without the support of my sister, Merry, who in some sense started me on this whole journey by picking up my call late one night and giving me the confidence to even imagine becoming an author. Throughout this entire process, she has been my most patient and sympathetic reader. I am lucky to have her as my sister and friend.

A wonderful circle of friends has shared and shaped this journey with me. Larissa de Lima deserves special thanks for nurturing this book into existence with her wisdom and care, and also for putting up with me through its ups and downs. Kousha Navidar inspired me by example to pursue something big and hard and creative, and sustained me during the tough periods with his honesty and humor. Lanre Akintujoye provided my first home base for the explorations in this book and believed in this project before I myself knew what I was exploring. Peter Buck has been a confidant, chef, distraction, inspiration, gadfly—my oldest, funniest, wisest mentor, and a true original. Simon Hedlin, Needham Hurst, Jillian McLaughlin, and Mark Weber alternately coached, cajoled, and cheered me on, giving me confidence, inspiration, and practical support.

The ideas in this book have benefited enormously from the wisdom of Deborah Brautigam, Calestous Juma, Sophus Reinert, Tang Xiaoyang, and Gunnar Trumbull. To have had the chance to be in a sustained dialogue of ideas with such incisive, open, and iconoclastic minds has been a privilege and joy in its own right. And beyond the realm of research and ideas, I've had the unique opportunity to work in the Africa-China space in the professional world. Particular thanks go to Jane Xing and Kartik Jayaram, mentors who have inspired me to believe ever in the possibilities of positive change even while challenging me to grapple with the realities of how the world works. Additional thanks go to my teammates and colleagues at McKinsey & Company, who not only put up with me while I was finishing the book but also teach me something new every day.

As the old saying goes, "It takes a village," but in my case, it has taken quite a few villages across the globe. Dimeji Bankole, Mark Bennett, Peter Buck and Deborah Wilkes, Jess Goldfin and Sean Flynn, Mario Lazzaroni and Wangechi Mutu, Brendan Lehnert and Lulu Wang, Elias Schulze, John Wagner, and Kerry Yang all generously took me into their homes while I was wandering around the world researching and writing. Robert Lawrence, Dutch Leonard, John Macomber, and Dante Roscini provided practical help and academic cover to write parts of this book while I was in graduate school. Mark Bennett, Loi Eng Koon, Salima Otaru, and Irene Wong provided valuable contacts and indispensable local knowledge. Nicole Summers and Munia Jabbar provided thoughtful and gracious comments on an early draft, and Deborah Brautigam and Yinuo Li (along with two anonymous reviewers) provided careful and insightful comments on a later one. Vanessa

Acknowledgments

Meng worked tirelessly to chase down many of the hard-to-find facts in the twisty territory through which this book meanders.

In writing this book, I have been lucky to work with a rock star editorial team that had the guts to take a chance on an unlikely idea and the skill to shape it into something to be proud of. Howard Yoon has been part agent, part writing coach, part ideas guru. His honest criticism and relentlessly high quality bar has made me a better writer. Jeff Kehoe has been my bedrock in the editorial process, full of patience and the wisdom not only of action but also of restraint. David Champion helped clarify my thinking on the overall argument, Martha Spaulding sharpened the text with her unmatched copyediting, Stephani Finks designed exactly the perfect cover, and Dave Lievens got the book over the finish line with patience and grace. Thank you to the entire team at Harvard Business Review Press—you have made this book better and been a true pleasure to work with.

A few final, indispensable words of gratitude. To my parents, Jin Shen and Hui Bin Sun: you are the most courageous people I know. It is fitting that my earliest memories involve journeys with you, for you helped launch me into a lifetime of exploration. To Sacha—my friend, my partner, my love—thank you for being the companion who shares every adventure, and the home at the end of every journey.

ABOUT THE AUTHOR

IRENE YUAN SUN is a leading expert on Africa-China relations. She co-leads McKinsey & Company's work on Chinese economic engagement in Africa and is the lead author of McKinsey's research report on this topic. She has helped multiple global organizations engage with Chinese policymakers and its private sector to advance the development of African economies. Her work has been featured in *Harvard Business Review*, *The Economist*, CGTN (formerly known as CCTV), Xinhua News, and the Nigerian *Guardian*.

Irene started her career by serving as a public school teacher in Namibia. She is a graduate of Harvard Business School, Harvard Kennedy School, and Harvard College.